GROWING UP ALEXANDER

GROWING UP ALEXANDER

My Life With a Psychoanalytic Pioneer

Ilonka Venier Alexander

KARNAC

First published in 2017 by
Karnac Books Ltd
118 Finchley Road
London NW3 5HT

British Library Cataloguing in Publication Data

A C.I.P. for this book is available from the British Library

ISBN-13: 978-1-78220-498-5

Typeset by Medlar Publishing Solutions Pvt Ltd, India

Printed in Great Britain by TJ International Ltd, Padstow, Cornwall

www.karnacbooks.com

"Don't brood on what's past,
But never forget it either."
Thomas Raddall

To Julia, to my cousins Eva and Ruth, Judit,
Vera and Robin, and Stella, and to
my grandfather, Big Papa.

CONTENTS

ACKNOWLEDGEMENTS

A number of people assisted over the years with the work needed to complete this project and deserve my gratitude. I wish to express my deep appreciation to those who, through either their suggestions, criticisms, and/or encouragement were helpful to bring this work to completion: Dr Jane Matson, Brian Oram, Dr Vera Alexander, Dr Judit Meszaros, Marla Horn, Beth Toomey, and especially to my husband of more than 20 years, Graham Benvie.

Dr Carl Bell and Dr Brett Kahr have been valuable contributors and through the process have become friends as well as mentors. This book would never have been finished without their involvement.

I wish to thank the editorial staff of Karnac Books for their ongoing assistance and advice. A special thank you goes to Cecily Blench. Once again, I must express my gratitude for the supportive publishing relationship with Karnac Books that has now spanned almost four years and resulted in three separate projects.

A very special debt of gratitude is owed to Julia Gunn for her collaboration, friendship, and support for more than 25 years. With her expertise in research, many insurmountable problems were resolved. None of this could have happened without her help.

FOREWORD

Professor Brett Kahr

Few memoirs have gripped me and moved me as much as this one.

Ilonka Venier Alexander, granddaughter of Sigmund Freud's most creative disciple Franz Alexander, grew up as "psychoanalytic royalty" with a "silver spoon in my mouth". Surrounded by considerable wealth and glamour, and schooled alongside the children of Hollywood's greatest movie stars, she enjoyed much material privilege. In theory, Ilonka Alexander had a perfect life.

Sadly, however, Ilonka endured considerable emotional deprivation and abandonment from many of her primary caregivers throughout childhood. A traumatised family who hid their Jewish identity to avoid the regnant anti-Semitism in Continental Europe, the Alexanders portrayed themselves as Gentiles, and little Ilonka grew up completely unaware of her family's Jewish ancestry. After her grandfather emigrated from Berlin to the United States of America during the early 1930s, he presented himself as Christian, married to an Italian Catholic grandee.

In spite of Franz Alexander's remarkable achievements and his contributions as a "progressive visionary", and as one of the most creative mental health professionals in world history, he interfered greatly in his granddaughter's life, and even offered Ilonka's father $50,000 to disappear so that he, Professor Alexander, could take charge of the young girl himself. As Ilonka admits, "I suffered and endured years of psychological abuse". Ilonka's own mother abandoned her at various points, as did her grandmother and, also, her aunt, creating confusion and sadness and, at times, despair.

As Freud taught us, beneath each "manifest content" of the dream lurks a more sinister, often darker "latent content". In many respects, the manifest content of Ilonka Alexander's life sparkled but its latent content seethed. As Ilonka writes in her memoir, "It would be years before I would learn that the women in my life were broken and therefore their responses to me were not normal. It was not my fault. I had done nothing wrong".

Remarkably, in spite of the depth of emotional deprivation, Ilonka mobilised her own considerable internal resources and, aided by good friends and by a sturdy psychoanalyst who offered professional assistance, she found an extremely creative way to work through and to survive some of the emotional traumata of her early life, and succeeded in embarking upon a fulfilling and innovative career as a clinical social worker and psychotherapist. Moreover, she forged a loving marital alliance with her husband. And, in later years, she traced her family's Jewish roots and managed to meet dozens of relatives whom she had not known previously. To top it off, she also became a most accomplished author.

This book will be of great interest to practitioners of psychoanalysis and to historians of psychoanalysis, many of whom have a long-standing interest in Franz Alexander and his work. But one need not be a mental health professional to benefit from this memoir. Ilonka Alexander has written this text with such honesty, such frankness, such transparency, such tenderness, and such emotional intelligence, that one cannot help but be moved and inspired. Unflinchingly and refreshingly honest, and generous as well, this autobiography offers a gripping reminder about the cost of the human struggle and, happily, about the many magnificent ways in which we can turn tragedy into triumph.

I would place this book on a par with such twentieth-century icons of autobiography as Maya Angelou's *I Know Why the Caged Bird Sings* and Jeanette Winterson's *Oranges Are Not the Only Fruit*.

Lovingly conceived, this text provides the reader with a wonderfully moving and cathartic experience and makes one proud, in the end, to be a human being.

CHAPTER ONE

The curse of wealth, privilege, and absent mothers

I am the granddaughter of Franz Alexander, noted psychoanalyst and student, friend, and colleague of Sigmund Freud, the father of psychoanalysis and thought by many to be among the most influential thinkers of the twentieth century, and perhaps the most important among them. Because of my grandfather's contributions to the field of psychoanalysis—some say he was the most important American analyst of the twentieth century, I am considered "psychoanalytic royalty". Ironically enough, my grandmother, Anita Venier Alexander, was truly noble and from an old Italian patrician family, the house of Venier. She and I are descended from three Venetian doges (Antonio Venier who ruled in the fourteenth century, Francesco Venier who ruled from 1554 to 1556, and Sebastiano Venier whose rule was more recent, in the seventeenth century) and her father was a count. She was raised in a convent school, outside Trieste, as was the custom for daughters of noble families. This practice was known as "giving the daughter up to the Church" and these girls were never expected to marry. The convent was administered by the Ancelle di Gesu Bambino which was established by Elena Silvestri in 1884.

It can be said that I was born with a "silver spoon in my mouth" though not in the traditional sense of those born into what we recognise and describe as "old money". The money my grandfather made after coming to America was substantial and was what can be considered "new money" though he would never be described as nouveau riche or garish. He was an intellectual aristocrat and there was nothing superficial or disingenuous about him. From an upper class European family, he was raised with the finer things in life, things he treasured; he passed on that appreciation to me, and he continued to enjoy these finer things in America and to share his largess with his children and me. (In recent years, however, it has come to light that he may not have been as generous with his own sister when she asked for assistance at the time she lost everything during the waning days of World War II in Nazi-ravaged Budapest. One sister said of him that money and America destroyed him and made him hard and insensitive. Freud sent him off to America with the fear that capitalism and materialism in America would ruin him. I never saw those negative qualities in him.)

The term intelligentsia was widely in use during the second half of the nineteenth century, mainly referring to better educated social strata in various countries. This historical intelligentsia in Eastern Europe, including Hungary, represented a cohesive phenomenon and my great grandfather, Dr Bernard Alexander, was right in the middle of it in Budapest as a professor of aesthetics and philosophy at the University of Budapest and a member of the elite and highly esteemed Hungarian Academy of Sciences. The Hungarian Academy of Sciences is the most important and prestigious scholarly society of Hungary and occupies prime real estate on the banks of the Danube in the capital city of Budapest. It was established in 1825 and its main responsibilities are to support scientific research and development and to be the steward of Hungarian accomplishments around the world. (Dr Bernard Alexander's son, Dr Franz Alexander, my grandfather, was also a member of the Hungarian Academy of Sciences as was Dr Alfred Renyi, grandson of Dr Bernard Alexander.)

Members of the intelligentsia had their own set of values, morals, and manners. These characteristics and a clear sense of etiquette were based on education which was the prime separator between the intelligentsia and the bourgeoisie. These values and manners were accompanied by and characterised by a compelling sense of calling or profession (*Development of Class Structure in Eastern Europe: Poland and Her Southern Neighbors*. Gella, Aleksander, Albany, NY, 1989, p. 130).

The values of this social class were strongly embedded in the childhood home of my grandfather, and his own father personified the nearly compulsive belief in the need to accept the mores and values of the social stratum in order to advance professionally and maintain important associations. These qualities were so engrained that Bernard Alexander invented a ruse to describe his own childhood and family to make his background sound more fascinating to his peers. He told the lie that his father had been abandoned, with a sole other sibling Rosa, at the steps of a church or orphanage after their mother had jumped into the Danube and died. Her husband was allegedly an army officer who deserted the family. The names of Bernard's parents were unknown. This story was passed on through succeeding generations until 2012 when it was discovered by his great granddaughter, the author, to be categorically untrue. In fact, genealogical records substantiate that Bernard was the oldest of six children, raised all together in Budapest, and his own father was present at the ceremony when he married Regina Broessler in Vienna in 1880. Until 2012 no Alexander family member was aware that Bernard's parents were Marcus Alexander and Julie Klein. This lie may also have been invented to deny Bernard's family's Jewish heritage during a time when Jews were persecuted in Hungary.

Paradoxically, the term strata did not carry with it an economic component. It was as if the difficulties of traditional economic class struggles were overcome and the intelligentsia considered itself free of such mundane burdens. As if, "above it all". Education at the gymnasiums was humanistic and thus produced gentlemen scholars. Along with a humanistic education came a disdain for mercantile occupations and the possible slow impoverishment of those young men of the gentry. (The concocted story of Bernard's parents may also have been to hide the fact his father spent some of his life as a Jewish retail shop owner in Budapest.) The educated intelligentsia had to accept their idealised elements of a traditional culture in order to establish and maintain their social status. My great grandfather, and my grandfather, too, considered themselves to be part of this old established culture and, therefore, the elite of Hungarian society. In this author's recently published memoir of Artur Renyi, *Love and Survival in Budapest*, Dr Franz Alexander's brother-in-law (married to his younger sister Borka) writes of establishing a home for their son that replicated the home created by Bernard Alexander for his children a generation earlier.

My grandfather left Europe for the final time in 1932 and brought his two children to Chicago with him. This was before the mass exodus of other Jewish analysts escaping Nazism and seven years before Freud left Vienna for England. He settled on the lake front and founded and ran the Chicago Institute for Psychoanalysis for twenty-five years, at which time he pressed further west to California. He described a lifetime of wanderlust and the need to always search for new places, new people, new challenges, and to repeatedly push personal and professional boundaries. He was creative and he had a brilliant mind, like his father before him.

It is no secret that having wealth can provide a person with status and power, and can open important doors to acquiring education and polish. With the benefit of adherence to healthy moral and personal values, the wealthy person will generally have a strong enough inner world to sustain the core needs for belonging, self-esteem, contribution to others, and love. In this case, wealth can be a great blessing. But when wealth subsumes

4

the self and substitutes for what we need on a deep, human level, it can become a Faustian bargain. And when you add to the mix psychological trauma in childhood, the end result can be catastrophic. This later description is what happened in the Alexander family. And it began many generations ago.

Children of wealth often begin life with prescribed identities and a sense of social and financial superiority; they are targets for jealousy and are often seen as a success by their peers simply for being born who they are. This can make it difficult to form a personal identity. The social world that their family likely occupies comes with an already established set of rules and expectations that the children of wealth are implicitly expected to buy into. And having too much of everything can undermine personal dreams as well. They may reason that they deserve no more and have no right to personal success of their own. They may give up their dreams before they get a chance to even formulate in their minds. Who are they to want anything when they already have so much? And, on the other side, why should they go through the tedious and frustrating experience of being on the bottom when they're already at the top? But it is often just this experience of being a worker among workers that the child of privilege needs and craves. Perhaps for me this need to be normal developed after my mother was told, because she was pretty, that she did not need to work for anything in life; men would rescue her and take care of her. This may have been the norm for beautiful women in 1930s and 1940s high society in the American Midwest. Later still, maybe this need to be normal or average, and to not exert herself mentally, drove my mother into a marriage to a grocery store produce man … the very embodiment of occupation that her intelligentsia father loathed. This man was her third husband before she reached the age of thirty-one. Or maybe she did so for the obvious shock value to her parents who were often described and felt by her to be interfering and demanding. However, in fairness, they were merely living up to the ideals and standards of their social standing and hoped that she would do so as well.

My grandfather expected his children to pursue academic careers as his own professor father had expected the same of him and his siblings a generation earlier. Though my grandfather quickly became assimilated into American culture, and began a very successful professional life with money and status, he held on to many if not all of his elitist Hungarian intelligentsia values. My mother had different ideas, and never excelled academically as he had hoped she would. She was more interested in a social life and did poorly at the expensive and posh private schools she attended. She had to repeat a US history class while in her junior year in high school and took the final exam by flipping a coin to determine her answers. She had already been told by her own mother that she need not work hard at her studies because she was beautiful and men would be attracted to her and would take care of her. She was not really encouraged to become independent or to achieve professional success. Yet my mother was exceptionally bright. Her knowledge of classic literature was extensive; her love and knowledge of classical music and opera were impressive. Oddly enough, though, she never studied or played a musical instrument and she never read books. (This did not stop me from giving her books at Christmas when I was an adult.) She eventually quit university after only two years and returned home to Chicago during the first year of World War II to work at the University of Chicago as a secretary, where she met my father. Whatever dreams she may have had were never shared with me or discussed with anyone else. In many ways her life, her dreams, her thoughts and beliefs were kept from me and others. Sadly, she was always an unknown to me.

Self-esteem is built through mastery of many small and large challenges, not merely innate. In wanting to prove themselves not necessarily as better but as good enough, the children of wealthy parents encounter the same fears of failure that any person trying to succeed does, though in their case, the stakes can feel much higher. What if they try and fail?

Entitlement is one of the most commonly cited qualities of the child of wealth. My own mother, her younger sister, and my grandmother as well, all had personality deficits that included entitlement although from very different childhood challenges and trauma. My grandmother was placed in a convent at the age of three and did not know her father who had perished in a duel prior to her birth. Her mother remarried soon after her birth and it can be interpreted that her mother chose her husband over her daughter (behaviour that was also chosen by my mother). These circumstances created in her what is known as borderline features: she was cold, demanding, impossible to please, and could neither show nor tolerate intimacy. She was a "bad" mother to her two children. My own mother had to endure a childhood with an absent father (who was busy building his psychoanalytic empire), and an absent mother as well, a mother who was cold and distant. My mother, a bit more psychologically healthy than my grandmother, can be said to have shown narcissistic features. My mother had secret feelings of insecurity, shame, vulnerability, and humiliation. To outsiders she appeared and acted carefree, happy, and the life of the party.

As a clinical social worker I know now that these are features of a personality disorder and this behaviour can be best labelled as superficiality. To feel better, Mama reacted with rage or contempt and often belittled me to make her own self appear or feel superior. She was often depressed and moody because of life circumstances or because I fell short of the perfection she needed from me. I always felt her disdain for and disappointment in me and never felt happiness or goodness from her. I spent my childhood and adolescent years afraid of her. And, of course, I was terrified of my grandmother who I saw as powerful and hurtful. I also think my mother and aunt were afraid of my grandmother from time to time; afraid of her rage, her rejection, and her hostility.

Entitlement and poor self-esteem do not always emerge when children of wealth have constantly had things magically appear, though my mother most certainly grew up with money and servants, and had an ostensibly easy life. I know that my grandfather, during my mother's adult years, continued to grease or smooth the path through her world in the hope that he could remove annoying obstacles that others more psychologically fit than she was had learned to cope with and accept. I believe now that this pattern was what he thought fathers should do for their children. However, I think this gave my mother the impression or lesson that she could not care for herself properly and that she was always going to fail. (This pattern first occurred when my parents divorced and my grandfather changed my name because he was assuming the father role. My mother had named me Nina Alexandra and my grandfather changed it to Ilonka Frances after both his older sister and himself.) Maybe failure and disgrace became an anticipated outcome for my mother and a behaviour that was carried into all situations. Sibling order here did not play much of a role in that she did not follow in her father's footsteps as other firstborns do. On the other hand, after floundering for years after undergraduate school, I did follow in my grandfather's footsteps as my younger half-sisters looked elsewhere, deliberately, for other roles to fill. Though a firstborn, I was not raised with my half-sisters and always considered myself an only child.

My mother may have learned to tolerate anything and everything from demanding, perfectionist, narcissistic parents who overvalued the money they earned in America while enjoying their status in Chicago's high society. Neither my mother nor I ever had the usual limits and constraints that a normal budget would impose. There was a constant flow of money while at the same time my grandfather was busy buying my mother out of parenting, by means of boarding school, while my mother turned the job over to hired people when it was time to come home from school every second or third weekend. I felt starved of my mother's love and time and infrequently had those needs met when my grandfather and grandmother flew to California from Chicago for a short visit. I had too little of the important things such as love and attention and too much of the material things and opportunities that money and position can provide. Coupling that with a boarding school experience, I had a cockeyed sense of what was "normal" to want, have, or expect. I always felt confused, not secure, and torn inside. I looked at my classmates, from intact families, and longed to be a part of that myself. When I was with my grandfather I felt safe and good. When I was with my grandmother or my mother, I felt inadequate and bad.

I grew up with high expectations placed upon me. I learned early on that the only chance to obtain love and approval meant I had to be the best, not merely do my best. There is a vast difference, and high regard came to me only with success and high achievement. I always felt the pressure to succeed in larger than life terms as I tried to reach an ever higher bar of success. Maybe those expectations were placed on me in an effort to make up for what my mother was unable to produce for my grandfather. Maybe I was considered a replacement daughter. I was expected to find activities that were meaningful and expected to do well whether it was riding a horse or learning another language during the summer holiday time. Eventually, but not until my twenties, I learned that the ability to choose could be both liberating and overwhelming, though I initially was afraid. I never felt as though I was allowed to make my own personal choices until I was in college and it was overwhelming and scary to me. All of us need to feel that we are making a meaningful contribution to the world in which we operate. We must be allowed to find our own path. That was and is an edict I live by.

People of wealth may want others to conform to their worldview rather than conforming to the other person's, to dance to their tune, so to speak, which can become controlling. The natural give and take and compromise of relationships can feel foreign to the wealthy person who is used to having things his own way all the time. We all know people who are used to getting what they want, when they want it, whether it's good food, services, or things. My mother had difficulty making friends in her generation and tended, at the end of her life, in her sixties and beyond, to make friends closer to my age. Interpersonal relationships were a challenge for my grandparents and my mother. They all seemed confused with the dynamics of intimacy. (Dr David Terman, the former director of the Chicago Institute for Psychoanalysis, told me in 2010 that nobody in Chicago knew anything about my grandfather's family or his personal decisions and choices. My grandfather most certainly had a personal side that he kept secret and a professional side that he showed to the public. They were not the same.) As is often the case in friendships, there would be an argument or a disappointment, and my mother could not tolerate those emotions. She would sever the relationship at that time and never look back. Friends, spouses, and children are not employees; they don't collect a pay packet and don't like receiving a bulleted list of tasks and objectives. Though the person of wealth cannot fire blood relatives like employees, he may fire them emotionally if they become too demanding, preferring the types of relationship where he is more in control, less challenged, and feels more "appreciated". This can especially be true of the person who holds all the important cards and is in the controlling or dominant position; why should he endure interpersonal disappointments when an adoring public gives him awards and does what they're told?

On the other hand, there is always what psychologist Carl Jung referred to as the "shadow" or the part of a person that is the submerged opposing aspect. The same person who feels overly entitled and impatient can have a shadow that feels small and anxious; he may feel guilty and out of balance and can yearn for someone to depend on, to "put him in his place" and feed him emotionally; the shadow side is the demanding part, where feelings of being insecure and undeserving live.

At the other end of the continuum reside the concepts of control and entitlement. One is either controlling or controlled, in or out of control. One can also either be entitled or feel undeserving. In personal relationships wealthy people may tolerate too much, their guilt allowing other people to use them and take advantage of them. My mother, most likely a narcissist, often took the path of least resistance and allowed others to blame her for things she did not do. Because she allowed her younger sister to blame her, instead of speaking up, my mother developed a rage and resentment towards her only sibling. Their relationship was never close.

Both Mama and my grandfather did whatever they could to avoid confrontation. They tended to have a hard time feeling and keeping personal boundaries and they had trouble saying no and yes. My mother often gave away precious and expensive family heirlooms and belongings to new-found friends, behaviour I consider inappropriate and wrong. She had problems around self-regulation that kept her from knowing what a "normal" relationship looked like. This was true for friendships and her relationships with her three daughters. Like her mother before her, she engaged in splitting behaviour and often spent years without communication between herself and one of her three children. (In fact, she left the author in California at seventeen when she moved to Reno and did not see her again until her firstborn was in her mid-thirties. She left her two small children with her ex-husband after a second divorce and did not continue a relationship with them, ever.) She often felt she deserved more and when disappointed, could not tolerate not receiving better treatment. She was entitled and controlling. My grandfather allowed my high-strung grandmother to create an atmosphere at home and with me that was filled with antagonism and animosity. He did not know how to set limits with her and accepted or tolerated her bad behaviour and looked the other way when her behaviour hurt him, her children, or me. I, however, was allowed no such indulgences in that I was expected to follow the norms set out by the intelligentsia when dealing with school, friends, and family.

All of these experiences represent confusion in thinking, feeling, and behaviour for young children. Growing up in a world of privilege can both open doors and close them. It can make the day to day work of developing a career and a relationship seem like too much work; when it doesn't happen easily, the child of wealth may want to give up. My own personal experience has been to immediately abandon whatever I attempted to do that did not go well, that is, perfectly. I once threw a bowling ball down a bowling alley. It did not hit as many pins as I thought it should. My way to cope with the embarrassment and humiliation of doing such a poor job in front of friends was to make the decision that I would never go bowling again. I once tried to make a dress and found a pattern too complicated to follow. I threw away the pattern and the expensive silk material and never attempted sewing again. I never roasted a chicken because I thought I did not know how, despite being an excellent cook with scores of cookbooks. I did not want to make a mistake. Making a mistake was to be avoided at all costs. Mistakes were not tolerated. It was drilled into me … mistake equals failure. Making a mistake was neither the way to learn nor to obtain approval or attention. As Vince Lombardi said, "Winning is everything."

Money was not valued in the home of Bernard Alexander and Regina Broessler. The Budapest home of my grandfather valued intellect and the pursuit of knowledge instead. However, it seems that after he came to America, Big Papa may have begun to change some of his ideas and in America today, in the twenty-first century, the worship of millionaires by some among us is at an all-time high. But when money becomes the only yardstick of success, it opens correspondingly the door to all sorts of problems that surround those essentially superficial and unimportant social values. Certainly my grandfather was thought of as the star of the family as he was able to command a high hourly rate as a psychoanalyst and was the most successful sibling in the family. He enjoyed his star status. He enjoyed his wealth and gave generously to friends and family.

As if almost a reaction formation, I have continued to embrace the values of my family three generations ago: the importance of intellect, the importance of feeling and expressing gratitude, and the importance of making a difference in the lives of those around us as well as society as a whole. You will see, these old norms and values also shaped my mother's life but perhaps in a negative way instead. A gypsy fortune-teller in Boston once told me when I placed my hands, palms up, for her to see, "Vast sums of money will slip through your hands." It is true. Money is certainly not the most important thing in my life. I understand it, I need it from time to time, but other values pushed me to achieve. It is those other values that moulded me, the values of my grandfather and his father before him, in Budapest's intelligentsia community, that are still front and centre.

Certainly I suffered and endured years of psychological abuse in a family directed by the famous Dr Franz Alexander, my Big Papa. And that word is right. Directed. He controlled and managed what people knew of the family and how decisions were made just as his father had done a generation before. Couple those difficulties with the fact that as a young child I learned I was neither lovable nor loved. The real tragedy, learned decades later, was that my own mother was herself not securely attached. It is no wonder she could not tend to my needs. But I am getting ahead of myself. Let's go back in time. Back to Chicago in the 1940s as we learn of how this most distinguished psychoanalyst interferes in his daughter's life and thus begins a lifelong pattern of family dysfunction for him and subsequent generations.

My grandfather sitting on the
balcony of the Palm Springs house.

My mother Silvia Alexander
as a young woman.

Dr Franz Alexander, who I called
Big Papa.

My father Dr George Julian
Rotariu.

My aunt, my father's mother, and my mother. Victoria Beaty,
Anna Rotariu and Silvia Alexander (Rotariu), left to right,
May 1944, Chicago.

New York Palace, home of the New York Life Insurance Company, where Dr Bernard Alexander and his wife Regina Broessler raised their children including my grandfather. Budapest.

CHAPTER TWO

The chaotic beginnings

My name is Ilonka Frances Venier Alexander though it was not always. I began my life as Nina Alexandra Rotariu, but that is a long tale and will be told later. I was born in Chicago during the last months of World War II and can be labelled a baby boomer; for the most part, much of my life's experience has been of that generation. What makes my story different and perhaps unique is the family into which I was born. My family is one of a world-famous psychoanalyst, a student, friend, and colleague of Professor Sigmund Freud, who made his own mark as a researcher, a scholar, an academician, a clinician, and can be called, in my mind, a progressive visionary. That may seem inflated or over the top but such are the words often used by others to describe him.

I always thought of Franz Alexander in superlatives. This giant of a man was my grandfather and I called him Big Papa. Big Papa adopted the role of my father. I assume the nickname was because I held him in such high regard and even as a child I knew he was an important man. I idealised him my entire life. In fact, I still do. He was for all intents and purposes my father and, in fact, suggested to my own father in an attempt to bribe him that he should stay away from me. I asked my father soon after I met him when I was twenty, "Why did you stay away?" His answer was that "Dr Alexander thought it was best.

He was the expert." And while he may have thought being raised without a father's important influence was perfectly alright for his young granddaughter, and so he stepped in, it was he who orchestrated the loss of my father in the beginning. My grandfather was initially and remained the only consistent male in my life and I knew him well. I was nineteen when he died. He started to shape my life from its very beginning.

That is where we should start, at the beginning. In order to get to the whole story we have to once again travel back in time to another era, travel to another century, and travel to another continent. We must journey to the past, to the Eastern Europe of the 1880s when my grandfather's parents were married in Vienna. The home that Bernard and Regina Alexander established in Budapest, into which Franz Alexander was born in 1891, was one of academic excellence within the intelligentsia of Hungary.

Those classified as intelligentsia, or the intellectual elite, had certain characteristics. They usually espoused moral beliefs or ideals that showed sensitivity towards their fellow man and were deemed to be advanced for the time. They generally insisted on continued self-knowledge. They shared an inescapable love of their own country. Their greatest inherent belief may have been of creativity, all developed with the aspiration for self-expression; a so-called finding of oneself. These are the ideas and ideals my grandfather grew up with in the home of his father, Dr Bernard Alexander, as the firstborn son after three daughters.

Bernard was a brilliant scholar, an expert on Shakespeare, and a philosopher with a post at the University of Budapest. He was active in the café society of Budapest and to his home came artists, musicians, writers, politicians, and other interesting and high achieving individuals. My grandfather saw all these personalities visit the home and yearned to participate in the discussions. He often hung out around the doorway to his father's library in order to overhear some interesting titbits.

When he was old enough, my grandfather was encouraged to discuss aesthetics, religion, philosophy, medicine, anthropology, archaeology, and psychology, but not with guests, with his father instead, the university professor. As I always looked up to my grandfather with awe, love, and respect, so too did he look up to his own father in this very same way. He nicknamed his own father the Sun King as he felt he radiated special light.

Bernard and Regina challenged their children to study, to learn, and to discuss their ideas with others. They encouraged intellectual pursuits and that ideal was the embodiment of success in this family as success in the Alexander family was not measured in financial terms. To attain success as an Alexander was much more refined and elusive. That state demanded much more of you than making money. In fact, gaining money for its own sake was considered low class or gauche. The achieving of success demanded strength of character, intelligence, a strong will, and a dedication to the ideals of the elite intellectuals who were so admired.

Nevertheless, my grandfather did achieve enormous financial success while pursuing the ideals set forth for him during his childhood and adolescent years at the knee of his professor father. My grandfather would become the more successful of the Alexander children, both financially and professionally, as he founded and led the Chicago Institute for Psychoanalysis through its first twenty-five years, years some say are the Golden Age of Psychoanalysis in America. He was considered the most brilliant one in the family and others hoped to realise similar achievements. He relished his status within the family and in the international psychoanalytic community, though he remained surprisingly insecure. When he died in March of 1964, several obituaries referred to him as the most important American psychoanalyst of the twentieth century.

After medical school, and a term in the Hungarian Army as a physician on a hospital train on the Italian front, my grandfather returned to Budapest to work. His work consisted of experiments in a lab at which time he became intoxicated with and interested in psychoanalysis. It was a stretch for him as he had thought his life's work would be in a lab investigating the mind-body connection through physiology. He would change focus when mind-body psychosomatics would ultimately become one of the cornerstones of his contributions during his long career.

He eventually decided to pursue an education as a psychoanalyst and moved to Berlin, with his wife, to become the first student at the Berlin Psychoanalytic Institute. He was the first student at the first training institute in the world. He savoured that designation and was proud to repeat it throughout his life. He would become the first visiting professor of psychoanalysis in 1930 when Robert Hutchins invited him to come to the University of Chicago, the first to establish an institute independent of a medical school, and the first to obtain large research grants. He seemed to enjoy his accomplishments. He particularly liked the designation and use of the word "first". He has been called grandiose by some, but I think that really meant that he seemed to others to be larger than life at times. He was a giant. He was a visionary and far ahead of his time. His mind, much like his father's, was brilliant, creative, and inquisitive.

In Berlin, in 1921, a first daughter, Silvia was born. Silvia was my mother. At that time my grandfather was nearly penniless. My grandmother supported the family with money earned translating movies and books. She was also a painter and eventually won a prestigious award in Germany. Soon, their scrimping and saving would end. Furniture pawned for money to live on would be reclaimed. Money would be plenteous even though Germany was in the grip of a depression. A second daughter, Kiki, was born in 1926. Big Papa was by now an outstanding researcher, writer, and clinician. His work rapidly became acknowledged through his writings and his speeches. He won the first Freud Prize.

During its adolescence, the psychoanalytic community had at its head, its leader and founder, Sigmund Freud. My grandfather had a close relationship with Freud who considered him the "hope for the future" and the one to "take psychoanalysis to America". Little did they know at the time, but Freud and Big Papa were distant cousins. This information has been unearthed with the assistance of genealogical research and the internet. My grandfather travelled to Vienna several times a year to see and spend time with Freud who was always eager to welcome him. Their friendship would continue through the early 1930s when my grandfather indeed did go to America and left his European background and extended family and siblings behind. Freud and my grandfather would write many very personal and intimate letters back and forth until Freud's death in 1939. Freud was worried that America would change Alexander; ruin him. My grandfather once said, "In Europe my professional life was an appendix to my personal life. Here I find the opposite is true; my private life has become the appendix." Looking back it seems to me that Freud had reason to be worried.

Analysts in the 1920s were so in awe of Freud and the basic concepts of psychoanalysis and were thus reluctant to criticise the master even the slightest bit. My grandfather, however, had his own ideas about how to interpret those concepts yet always considered himself to be a Freudian analyst. He, did, nonetheless, want to be on his own and not "sit at Freud's knee" as he referred to his dreams in a 1950s interview with Dr Kurt Eissler. He did not want to merely pay homage to Freud forever. My grandfather was intensely curious and creative, traits learned and nurtured by his professor father whom he idolised and wanted to impress.

Some would criticise my grandfather, then and in more modern times, for what they thought was his abandonment of Freud. However, actually he did no such thing. He simply had his own way of looking at the basic beliefs of Freud's psychoanalysis and these ideas are well documented in his many books and articles as well as his legacy at the Chicago Institute for Psychoanalysis and in the fields of psychosomatics and psychoanalysis, psychotherapeutic theory and treatment.

My mother Silvia was raised with privilege and financial extravagance. She attended private schools both in Germany, before moving to America, and in Chicago. Clothes came from the most expensive stores, the family lived in the most exclusive neighbourhoods in Chicago, had a summer home in La Jolla with its own private beach, and they had live-in help. Silvia was quite intelligent yet was unable to achieve the academic standards of excellence expected of her by her parents. Her mother, my grandmother, told her that she did not have to worry about achieving academic greatness because she was pretty and men would come to take care of her. She was considered to be a perfect daughter: beautiful and a carbon copy of her noble-born mother in terms of her patrician looks. It is said she married young to escape the domineering home life she detested and, naturally, the marriage did not last. She became pregnant with me despite her mother's rebuke to "not get pregnant" upon learning of the civil marriage ceremony in January of 1943.

My father was born in Los Angeles in August of 1917 to immigrant parents who had come from a part of the Austro-Hungarian Empire that is now Romania after Hungary lost land as a result of World War I. A second child, Victoria, was born in March 1920 and soon thereafter the family moved to the south side of Chicago where my paternal grandfather set up business in his own barber shop. While living in California my father's parents were told that the south side of Chicago was a good place for immigrants to reside and create a home for children. My father and aunt both excelled academically during their school years. My father enrolled in the University of Chicago during the war to study chemistry and physics. He was tall, handsome, charming, and engaging. He was friendly and easy to talk to and his family was generous, kind, welcoming, and warm. They were, however, not highly educated and not fluent in English at the time. Their son, George Julian Rotariu, was not considered to be of the right social standing to marry my mother, another immigrant, but one from a very different social stratum. My mother was from the intelligentsia and my father was bourgeois. And my mother's mother was strong-willed, outspoken, and controlling. My grandfather was consumed with his career and doing the right thing in order to succeed and assimilate. His plan for success did not include having a son-in-law whose parents were immigrants.

Soon after my birth, though my father told me that as a young couple he and my mother were happy, my mother left my father and succumbed to her parents' interference. Ironically, my parents remained in love with each other for decades and continued to talk from time to time. My mother told me in the early 1990s that she was sorry she allowed my grandparents to interfere in her life and that she knew that interference had made my life very difficult. When she apologised to me I was in my late forties. It was the first and only time she ever mentioned leaving my father, while other questions about him, their early married life, how they met, and her other partners were always unanswered. Despite being a psychoanalytic family, things were just not discussed, information was hidden or withheld, and important secrets were kept. Mama did admit at that time, in retrospect, that the decision to leave and divorce my father had been a huge mistake. In retrospect I believe such an admission most likely was difficult for her. In that moment, as a recent graduate from clinical social work school, I was proud of her revelation to me.

I was the first grandchild and named Nina Alexandra by my parents. I was born a month early when my mother became ill with toxaemia. When my parents separated, I was three or four months old and had not yet been baptised. My mother moved back home with her parents as many young women still do and most certainly did in 1945. My grandmother insisted on baptism and my grandfather said that if he was now going to support me, he would name me. I was baptised in March 1945 as Ilona Frances Alexander. Ilona was my grandfather's oldest sister who died tragically prior to his birth and Frances was the female version of his first name, Franz. My grandfather effectively claimed me as his own and my mother must have interpreted this as another failure in his eyes: an inability to name her child properly, perhaps parent her child, and the need for him to take over. She already knew that she had failed him when she was unable or disinterested to pursue an academic career. My grandfather announced that my father no longer existed and his name was never to be spoken in my presence. He offered my father $50,000 to stay away from me and my father agreed to keep away yet, to his credit, he refused the financial offering. It was almost fifty years later when I would learn of this event. I was horrified and shocked. Keeping my father from me was one of my grandfather's biggest mistakes. In so doing, however, he assured that role of father for himself. That decision set up for me a lifetime of insecurity and searching for a replacement father figure when he died in 1964. I, like others who saw his youthful zest for life, thought he would live forever.

I always saw my mother as a sad person. I think now that the light in her eyes must have gone out after the divorce from my father and the continued disappointment she felt from my grandparents: not finishing college, choosing an inappropriate partner, and the loss of Nina to Ilonka when my name was changed. It is no wonder she did what she knew best and what came easy for her. She found another suitor and married again, in La Jolla, a man who lived across the street from the Alexander summer home. After a few years in La Jolla, this man accepted a position as an aeronautical engineer with McDonell Douglas in Santa Monica. A year later the family broke up. But, I am jumping ahead in the story.

This man, Douglas Nigel Thomas (who I have since referred to as "my Thomas father"), must have been considered more palatable to the Alexanders' tastes and expectations than Mama's choice for her first husband. His father Benjamin was British and had designed the world famous Curtiss JN-4 "Jenny" aircraft used in the First World War before coming to America and settling in upstate New York where his two sons were born. Benjamin's wife died young and he was left to raise the two sons, which he did alone. Ironically, his son would do the same thing a generation later, raise two children alone without remarrying.

When Mama married Nie (my childhood nickname for him), the wedding photographs were sent to family around the globe and back in Chicago an article and photo appeared on the society pages headlined "Miss Alexander weds Douglas Nigel Thomas on the west coast." No wonder years later cousins would tell me they thought this was my mother's first marriage. With this photo and announcement, my father was erased and perhaps I was, too. This was not the first instance of manipulation or bending of the truth that would have dire consequences. I think he acquiesced to my grandmother who really wanted to believe that her firstborn had found, at last, a more suitable husband. My grandmother could be persuasive and my grandfather disliked disagreements. I am certain that my grandfather meant no harm, but he did do harm; immeasurable harm not only to his daughter, but to me, his granddaughter.

Memory is said to develop very early in life. Some say they are able to remember back to their second or third year. My memories of early childhood were always blotchy and somewhat inconsistent. I remember my adoptive father pretending to be Santa Claus on the roof of his father's house in La Jolla. This means I must have been about five or six as we had already left La Jolla for Beverly Hills. I do not remember my friend in the La Jolla preschool for whom my half-sister Marguerita was named. I remember my mother filling baby bottles for my sister in 1948 as I tugged at her skirt for attention. I was nearly four and this may be my first memory of her not being attentive to my needs as I tried to gain her response. It seems I spent a lifetime trying to get my mother's attention and approval as it appears to have started early. I remember my younger half-sister's birth in June of 1950. I was not yet six. I recall my mother slamming the door on my foot as I emerged from her Packard car being dropped off at school. I was in the first grade. I do not remember any of the times spent together as a family and when I first saw photos of these times in the spring of 2016, it was as if I was looking at the pictures of strangers. I do not recall my mother taking me away from my Thomas father and my younger sisters though my younger sister remembers vividly our departure and being left behind as Mama and I drove away. Not only had my mother not felt a bond with me, she had formed none with her other children either.

My Thomas father was allegedly "in love" with me as a child and eager to adopt me after he married my mother. My aunt says that he often joined her to babysit me when my mother went out on dates. He was my aunt's friend before he was officially introduced to my mother and set up on a date. He became my legal father when my biological father signed away his parental rights because "Dr Alexander thought it would be the best thing for you." My father told me this time and time again as if to justify his complete non-involvement in my life. Even as an adult he would often say to me, "I am not your legal father." I never really understood his need to repeat this to me as I saw it only as an excuse. I write this because my Thomas father and mother fought in divorce court for custody of us three girls for over eighteen months. Apparently both parents wanted all three children. At the last minute, before another court appearance, my mother told me he said he would concede to the divorce if he could have custody of his two biological girls. She agreed. This created confusion for all of us. If he was so keen on me, why use me as a bargaining chip? My mother agreed to the conditions and walked away from her younger children. There was no contact between us for almost a decade. I never understood this nor did my younger sister Marguerita. It is important to remember that in 1951 or 1952 it was most unusual for custody of two very young girls to be granted to a single father. Nearly all court decisions were made to favour the mother.

This was my fifth move in six and a half years as I was introduced to a second stepfather whom she married just days after her second divorce. Mama had married a man who had obviously been in the wings, waiting. When I learned of this exact timeline in 2015 I was filled with disgust and anger. I am certain my grandparents were bewildered as my mother married a grocery store clerk whose mother was oddly enough a member of the Daughters of the American Revolution. This stepfather was George Daniel Gray, another man named George. He was referred to in the family as George number 2 in order to differentiate him from my own biological father, George number 1.

It was sometime between my first and second year of school when my mother and I moved from our family home in what is now Century City bordering on Beverly Hills to a small apartment on Levering Avenue in Westwood Village. We left behind my two sisters. I have no memory of the family break-up or the move. What I do recall is my grandparents coming to visit and the fun we all had at the Bel Air Hotel, splashing in the pool, and eating at big round tables near the water's edge. I remember a kind lifeguard taking the time to teach me how to swim in that large circular pool. I do not know if a divorce was discussed or if custody issues were discussed as I was way too young to be involved in the discussions and rightly so. Soon thereafter I was just taken away, again, from my mother and placed in the boarding school at this time, "for my own good" and most likely for hers too. My poor mother continued her lifelong journey of not measuring up or meeting the hopes and dreams of her parents.

Each of these three daughters needed her mother's love and for me it would be a driving force throughout most of my life. My mother not being emotionally and later physically available had no effect on my striving to obtain her love and attention. It was as if I dragged her around my whole life yet I sought to be rid of her. It would be years later that I accepted that the one person who is supposed to love me without condition didn't. I began to try to cope as a young child, not really grasping the significance of what was happening around me. The healing came decades later. The understanding or belief that I was unloved affected all parts of my life but especially my relationships. I did learn though, eventually, that I was unlike my mother in that I had the ability to love and be loved. That key dissimilarity distinguished me from my mother. I learned it from my father's sister who I did not meet until I was nineteen, just one week after my beloved Big Papa died in March of 1964.

Memories of George number 2 are scant as I was away at boarding school most of the time or shunted away with his parents. I do recall George number 2 had a temper and often he would hit me on the head so hard that my hearing was lost for a day or two. I never told my mother as I knew she would not believe me nor would she protect me. This would occur when my mother was at work during a Saturday and I was left alone in the house with him. I did not like him nor did I like his parents. I remember he got angry at me for scouring a cast iron frying pan. I knew no better at eight years old. He became angry when I did not understand how to light a gas oven and allowed the gas to flow into the range before striking a match. Of course it blew up in my face, burned my face, and took off my eyebrows. He really got mad at that time. I think that is the first time he hit me in the ear.

Although I longed for my mother's attention and was eager to go home for the weekend from boarding school, I soon hoped the weekends would pass quickly and the bus would come to take me back to Chadwick School, my real home on the hill. I spent a lot of my childhood wishing away time. While with my mother, all I really wanted was to return to Chadwick and my friends. I wanted to be taken back to safety and security. After all, isn't that why I was placed there in the first place, because my mother had a major deficit in the mothering department?

My grandfather was right to remove me from my mother's care. In retrospect this decision to place me away from my mother and in a boarding school saved my life. Whatever personal or professional success I have been fortunate to achieve is a direct result of the care I received at the hands of Commander and Mrs. Chadwick.

Silvia Alexander with baby Ilonka, Chicago.

Ilonka on patio of La Jolla house, 1945.

Ilonka with her "Thomas father" Douglas Nigel Thomas and her younger half sister Marguerita Young. Photo taken in Century City spring 1950.

Ilonka with her half sister Marguerita Young, Century City, early 1950.

House at 2081 Kerwood Avenue in Century City, 1950.

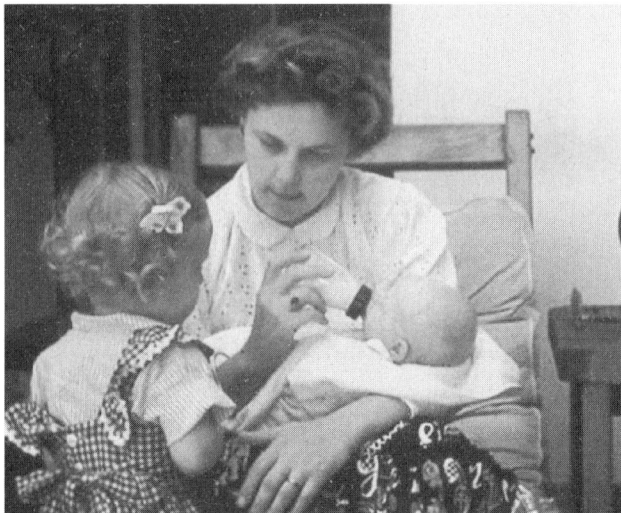

Ilonka's mother Silvia Alexander (Thomas) holding her youngest daughter Pennie (Woolf) with Marguerita looking on. Photo taken in patio of Century City home summer 1950.

Kerwood House, 2016.

Anita Alexander, Ilonka's grandmother, with her two daughters, Silvia and Francesca (Kiki). The photo was taken in the mid-1930s in Chicago.

La Jolla house built in the 1930s by Ilonka's grandparents. This house sits on the corner of Dolphin Place and Chelsea Drive on a double lot that Ilonka's grandmother purchased impulsively during her first trip to Southern California. This is the house where Ilonka learned to walk and talk.

CHAPTER THREE

Rolling hills, horses, surfers, and dolphins

My mother attended private schools and most of her cousins did as well. It was the norm for upper class intelligentsia parents to send their children off to private boarding schools. When it became clear to my grandfather that my mother was unable to provide a suitable environment for me, that she was unable to parent me effectively, he went looking for a new home, a home that would provide structure and consistency in an academic setting. Parenting concepts were foreign to my mother as she was impulsive and thought mainly of herself. She was unable to form an attachment to me and did not consider my needs, as a young child, at all. My grandfather researched all the schools in the southern California area and chose a private boarding school much like those my mother's cousins attended in the US and in Europe. Chadwick School was to become my adoptive mother and long-term home away from home.

Pop culture sometimes paints boarding schools in a way that isn't necessarily accurate or favourable. While the depictions are exaggerated examples of what the reality of boarding school life is truly like, films, TV, and books have left people asking and wondering: why would anyone want to go to a boarding school? Why would parents make the decision to place their children out of the home? And particularly, why place a child in a boarding school at such a young age?

Well, boarding school simply isn't always like the movies. It's an opportunity for students to learn a number of life skills while having access to a high-quality education. But one still asks, what are the benefits of boarding school? Again, why send your child to a boarding school and not a public school education while still living at home?

Boarding schools offer a variety of benefits to students. The decision to attend boarding school is the first step in what many consider a "big picture" consideration: by attending boarding school, the advantages that come with it will pay off in the long term. The number of leaders and successful members of society who began their journey at a private school is impressive: former presidents and other politicians, actors, athletes, and successful business people.

However, what makes most boarding schools work well is the vast number of extra-curricular activities, programmes, and challenges available to students on a daily basis. The successful boarding school student is one who wants to embrace this huge opportunity: to live in a community where learning, personal growth, and exploration are top priority; where non-academic programmes and activities are abundant; where making friends is paramount; and where success is celebrated. I see it now as a kind of extension of the supportive and educational home in which my grandfather was raised.

With all that said, in the long run, independence and self-sufficiency might be the greatest gifts that parents can give to their children. Away from home, we were required to navigate through the elements of boarding school life, do our own laundry, keep our personal space neat and tidy, and get up in the morning in time for breakfast before classroom work begins. Parents aren't there to shield their children from natural causes and effects. Boarding schools are good places to fail and succeed—which makes them great places to learn. It's a template of a controlled kind of freedom.

After boarding school, kids don't just get accepted into the college of their choice: they arrive prepared to succeed with the ability to manage their own lives. They become strong individuals capable of leadership and have self-initiative. The current state of our culture in North America has made it difficult for parents to cultivate those traits and private school is a channel for these important qualities to be nurtured. Students don't just have to manage their own affairs, they learn how to live and deal with other people. They are challenged to develop their interpersonal skills because there is no hiding at boarding school.

A child who is dropped off in the morning and picked up by a parent at three o'clock isn't challenged to develop the same peer skills as a kid who lives with other students twenty-four hours a day on campus. Boarding school is a transformative experience in learning to communicate with others, something a lot of people don't get until college, if at all.

"You probably won't have seventy siblings at any point during your lifetime, but at boarding school you do," said one Chadwick friend long ago, and that is exactly how I felt. As an only child at home, I felt alone and isolated. I had few friends in the neighbourhood though I had a good friend who lived next door. I did not have a loving family environment and I had no support system. At Chadwick I felt part of a larger entity, a family away from home, unlike anything I had at home, and we were all in it together. We were buddies, we supported one another, and the older high school students befriended those of us in the lower grades: we shared in common the mistaken impression that we were enrolled there in order to not be a nuisance at home. Most of us at the time loved the community atmosphere created at Chadwick. It's a bond that binds men and boys, women and girls, of different ages and cultures. It was only in my adult years that I came to appreciate that there was more to the boarding school decision than being out of the way or liberating my mother.

Chadwick, then and now, sits atop a large hill in Rolling Hills, California on the Palos Verdes Peninsula and became a community independent from the City of Los Angeles in 1957. I recall driving up the hill for the first time with faint memories of another important hill, the hill upon which the house in La Jolla sat. That house was on Dolphin Place overlooking the Pacific Ocean with a private beach below the cliffs. The La Jolla house is where I learned to walk and talk. It was where my earliest memories were created and the house has always been a beacon of light to me, then and now, reminiscent of only happy times, when my grandparents, my mother, and I lived together in harmony.

Rolling Hills has a rural and equestrian look to it, as it did in the 1950s, and there are no traffic lights. Properties have several acres of land with ample space for horses and sprawling homes. Wide horse trails course down the middle of Palos Verdes Drive North, stretching from Malaga Cove up through the homes closer to the school. Most homes are single-storey nineteenth-century California ranch houses or Spanish haciendas exemplified by architect Wallace Neff and are required to be painted white. Homeowners are also required to maintain horse stabling or, at the very least, keep land aside where horse stalls could be built by subsequent owners.

Until the 1980s the school owned the entire hill, from Palos Verdes Drive winding up to the top of the hill. The lower part of the acreage was sold off at that time to establish the school's endowment fund. (When I attended Chadwick there was no financial aid; now more than 50 percent of those attending receive some financial assistance. Tuition, then as now, is quite expensive.) The Palos Verdes Peninsula is surrounded by the Pacific Ocean and from the top of the hill at Chadwick one could see Redondo Beach and the stretch of sand reaching north, up to the airport. The hills were verdant and empty of structures.

I remember on weekends we were allowed to hike through the hills and to the top of the mountains and look beyond. The view was magnificent and the beaches were full of surfers showing off their skills before this sport became popular. I was mesmerised by the athletic skill of the men on their boards and became fascinated with surfing and the beach at that time.

The early years spent at Chadwick School in Palos Verdes Estates atop rolling hills, overlooking surfers below, provided me the most vital lessons, those of friendship and academic achievement. Friendships have always helped me overcome challenges and difficult tasks. Chadwick also provided stability and security, important features for childhood that my mother was unable to deliver. At Chadwick I could be seen and heard and appreciated. I never wanted to leave.

The school was founded in 1935 by Margaret Lee Chadwick and her husband, Commander Joseph Chadwick and was located in San Pedro, California. San Pedro is close to the port of Los Angeles and if you circle around Portuguese Bend by car from Chadwick you will arrive at San Pedro. Three years later the school moved to its current location. In the early days, Chadwick was an open air day and boarding school for seventy-five students from kindergarten to year 12. Initially open air schools were seen as a method of educating children with TB while providing them with fresh air, rest, and nutritious food. The movement emerged after World War I and diminished in the 1930s. However, Commander and Mrs Chadwick felt that children could best learn if allowed open space, small classes, and a structured and supportive environment akin to family, and they modified the open air concept when designing and executing their views about a day and boarding school. The dormitories were small and fewer than ten of us lived together. In the beginning I was in the third year and my dorm mates were younger than me and as old as the sixth grade. The emphasis was on individual instruction. Academics were important but when students get together after they've graduated and moved on to university and then successful careers, it's not the great history class they remember, but their time in the wilderness, the dorm life, or other memorable moments.

I was enrolled by my grandfather as a third grader in September 1952 and thus began my life living apart from my mother. And accordingly, this began my mother's formal abdication of her parental responsibility. In retrospect, as an adult looking back at the child I was, being away from the so-called support system of family and a few neighbourhood friends, and considering the challenges of becoming acquainted with this new place and a different style of learning, I realise that it actually did impose a heavy burden on me and exact a heavy toll.

Boarding school offers the opportunity for students to foster intense connections with their teachers, in part due to smaller, more intimate class sizes. The outlook of teachers at boarding schools regarding their position isn't that of a job, but more of a vocation, where they become an important role model in each of their students' lives. The teachers worked with us, shared meals with us in the large cafeteria, and often lived on campus, making it a difficult environment to duplicate anywhere else.

My Chadwick boarding school life was a reassuring environment and I took good advantage of those connections and the family-type environment. My boarding school teachers fully supported me in the endeavours and projects I wanted to take on. It was, as it turned out, the best preparation for life after school. While the educational experience at the boarding school is important to personal and educational growth and development, it's also a precursor to life after school. The burden for students graduating from private schools, while still apparent, is far more manageable than it is for public school graduates. During my teen years I felt more independent and self-sufficient than most of my friends and I attribute that development to Chadwick.

Research has shown that boarding school students feel more prepared for college and university than their peers, and are more likely to earn more advanced degrees like a master's or PhD, and advance to more prominent roles in their careers and communities.

At Chadwick I excelled academically and had many friends. I learned how to make and keep friends and those friends helped me manoeuvre through the difficult days. Days when my mother did not show up to visit. Days when my mother did not come to drive me home for the weekend. My classmates were mostly the children of celebrities and some of my good friends, Hoagy Carmichael Jr and Robert Walker Jr, were older than me. The children of actors Brian Donlevy, Ronald Reagan and Jane Wyman, and the Andrews Sisters were my friends. My best friend at Chadwick, Judy Reynolds, was the daughter of the school nurse who also lived on campus. My maypole dancing partner was Rocky Brynner, son of actor Yul Brynner who had just secured the Academy Award for his role in *The King and I*. My boyfriend in the seventh grade was the son of Oscar winning actress Susan Hayward, Gregory Barker. Greg's twin brother Tim and I ran for student council in the seventh grade and won. I spent many after-school hours swimming in the pool as my dream then was to be an Olympic swimmer. I was in the fourth and fifth grades and wanted desperately to be on the swimming team when I entered upper school in the ninth grade. I participated in school drama productions and began to learn the piano from a Frenchman named Pierre when I was in the third grade.

The piano and I seemed to be born for one another. I have a good ear and learning to play the piano came effortlessly. I already had some success in the third grade with foreign languages. I practised diligently and was habitually indoors conscientiously playing scales while friends played outside, climbed trees, or roamed the forest on the top of the hill. The piano recitals were held once a year in the auditorium of the school and the order in which the students played was based on ability. I usually played my choices near the end of the performances though I was much younger than many of the students who played after me. I had ability and I was a good student. Pierre was an excellent teacher. I never had any family member hear me play the piano. My mother never came to see me play. We did not even have a piano at home. She never expressed any interest in my ability yet that did not stop me from trying to get her attention. Looking at it now, I realise I must have thought if I did a good job, she would be interested to come and listen. I was wrong. The only ones cheering me on were Pierre and the dorm mothers and, of course, my friends. My need for Mama's attention and recognition now seems so pitiful and immature.

Love and friendship did not come from my mother. She was incapable of such emotions yet I naturally blamed myself. I constantly thought if I tried harder and harder, and did a more perfect job, she would be interested to either spend time with me or come to see me at school. She did none of those things. She preferred to spend time with her friends, acting the fool among men, flirting, and behaving childishly. She liked being the centre of attention. She was pretty and she liked playing that part at social gatherings. I must have been a reminder to her of responsibilities she neither wanted nor enjoyed. I did not truly live with her during those years even though there was a room in the house for me. I spent the majority of my time at boarding school and the other time at her in-laws' home, older adults who would have preferred a grandchild of their own instead of this ersatz granddaughter of European descent they were asked to provide a home for from time to time. I can only imagine how it galled them to care for me during those years.

This pretend grandmother was Gail Bowdoin Gray, from the established Bowdoins of Maine, whose arm of the family had moved west to the gold and silver mining towns in Colorado, and she now lived in Southern California. Gail's family founded Bowdoin College in Brunswick, Maine in the later decades of the eighteenth century. From its founding, Bowdoin College was known to educate the sons of the political elite and catered very largely for the wealthy conservatives from the state of Maine. Gail's political ideology was old school. She was a member of the DAR (Daughters of the American Revolution) and was most verbal about her disapproval of my mother and her European parents. Her only child, a son, had served with distinction in the US Navy during World War II and his black and white photo, in his dress uniform, was displayed prominently on the TV in the sitting room. No doubt his parents were displeased when he married for the first time a woman for whom this would be a third marriage. I wonder if they were able to overlook this and concentrate on my mother's psychoanalyst father instead. I seriously doubt it. I hated spending time with them and yearned for my mother to come and save me from this drudgery and altogether negative place. She never came. I kept on wishing, though, ever optimistic. I then began to truly wonder what was wrong with me that it seemed nobody wanted to spend time with me: either this make-believe grandparent family or my own mother.

As stated previously, I did not like my mother's choice of husband either. He was George number 2 to me though I did not know why at the time; I merely called him what I heard my mother refer to him, as when talking with my grandfather or my aunt Kiki. He was stern, harsh, cold, and an exacting disciplinarian. I dare not do anything that may cause him problems for he would strike me. He was cruel and my mother could be too. In the early years he and my mother came to visit me at Chadwick on my birthday. I was playing with friends and not in the dorm when they arrived. When I came back to the dorm, most likely later in the afternoon, I found the cake with this note, "You were playing. We are busy. We could not wait. Happy Birthday." One weekend home from Chadwick I recall that I got my period for the first time. She had never sat down with me to discuss menstruation or anything else for that matter. I knew nothing about these physical changes and my mother had done nothing to prepare me. When I noticed blood on my underwear, I summoned my mother to the bathroom. I suppose she provided me with supplies, I do not remember. What I do remember is going back into my room, a room that shared a wall with her bedroom, when I could hear Mama tell her husband what had happened though I had begged her not to tell. I heard them laughing. How I wished that the world would open up and swallow me then and there. I think I was thirteen at the time.

During the days at Chadwick I enjoyed horseback riding at the riding club near the school in Portuguese Bend. I enjoyed swimming and, as stated previously, dreamed of becoming an Olympic swimmer even though I was still too young to be part of the school's swimming team and to gain needed experience. The school's mascot is a dolphin and I most certainly felt part of the school community. The school was family to me. I wanted to participate athletically as a member of the dolphin swim team. I was good at languages and when I was in the seventh grade longed to be an interpreter at the United Nations. I enjoyed my classes; I got good grades, had friends, and was a class officer in middle school. I was the leader of my Girl Scout troop and spent many weekends away with friends and their families. My friends mainly lived on the Westside of Los Angeles in the swanky neighbourhoods of Beverly Hills, Holmby Hills, Brentwood, Bel Air, Westwood Village where we lived, and some of the canyons like Mandeville and Stone Canyon on the way to the Palisades where I would later live with Kiki as a college student. The dorm mother and I became friendly and she let me wash her car. Perhaps I inherited my love of cars from my mother and grandmother who both drove expensive and impressive cars (my mother drove a 1957 Thunderbird and my grandmother a Jaguar coupe). I climbed trees, explored the acreage at Chadwick, and spent a lot of time outdoors.

Not everything was fun and games, though. The importance of regulations and order was stressed. As a third grader I was expected to make my bed and the area in the bedroom neat and tidy before going to the cafeteria for breakfast. If the bedcovers were not tight enough to bounce a quarter, the bed was stripped. Just like that. I soon learned how to make a tight bed with correct hospital corners. There was a system for demerits and the chance to win back lost ones. We were not allowed much candy or snacks and all our money was left for purchases in a canteen-like store. Sometimes I could hear the dorm mothers spank other students with a paddle and I could hear crying from my bedroom. I do not recall this ever happening to me.

One of the earliest memories of being bullied and scared was when Chris Crawford, the son of actress Joan Crawford, would hide and frighten us. Chris was older than me and lived in another dorm, closer to the cafeteria and one that I had to pass daily. At night he would shoot some kind of gun that released wooden matches that sailed past us while we walked to the cafeteria in the dark for dinner. My fear of the dark and the bogeyman began at that time and continues to this day. If I am alone in the house, I am unable to sit without many lights turned on. I would never take a walk in the dark, even in the sleepy little village where I live. I try to not drive at night and I would never drive alone at night.

For the most part Chadwick was a very positive experience. I wished for school to start during the summer months when I missed the routine, my friends, and wanted to be away from the Grays. When I was in the sixth grade and told my mother I wished the summer would end, it was too long, she said that I should not wish my life away. I did not know what she meant at the time but I do now. I was wishing for a change in the only way my young child's mind could fathom.

But for reasons never told to me, I had to leave Chadwick. I was not involved in any discussion nor was I informed before school started that I would not be returning to boarding school for the next year. I was told I would return to the household of my mother and her third husband where I had a room but did not live. Soon afterwards this arrangement would also change and the family would have my grandfather at the helm and I knew he would watch over me. Other than knowing that, I have no memories of what I thought or felt about these modifications in terms of my awkward relationship with my mother. In fact, through most of my life the memories are incomplete and negligible.

Old sign and gate into Rolling Hills, California.

The Commander and Mrs Margaret Chadwick stand in front
of the opening gate to Chadwick School. The sign outlines the
ideals of the school.

Third grade class at Chadwick School 1953. Ilonka sits to the
far left in the first row.

CHAPTER FOUR

The teen years … Big Papa to the rescue

Sometime during my ninth grade in school, and just after leaving Chadwick, my mother's third marriage broke down. Of course, I knew nothing of what was transpiring, had never seen or heard arguments, or felt their discontent (how could I, I did not live with them full time), and was surprised when, all of a sudden, we were moving again. This move meant that my survival was to be placed in the hands of my grandfather and I would be able to seek my emotional needs from him.

When my mother's marriage broke down I was happy to learn that we would leave behind the Grays permanently. I knew I would never again be exposed to their disapproval and their unspoken desires that another child should be in their home instead of me. It never occurred to me at the time that another move would also mean more chaos, the challenge of making new friends, and an adjustment to an alternative school after so many years, happy years, at Chadwick. However, when my mother told me that we would be moving in with my beloved grandfather, Big Papa, I was ecstatic and pleased. All of a sudden I had something to look forward to and I hoped for good times for my mother as well. As I revealed earlier, I was always hoping for a different ending with my mother, a close mother-daughter relationship. I know now that this is what therapists call magical or crazy thinking. I call it wishful thinking.

In an excerpt from a poem written to the first graduates from Chadwick School in 1940, Margaret Chadwick said,

> The bang of the heavy door
> Marks your brave entrance to a struggling world.
> Gird fast your shining youthful armour,
> Hold fast your shining youthful dreams,
> Give to mankind the vibrant tumult
> That is you.

This certainly reflected my feelings at this important time, a major turning point, in my life. This philosophy would guide and drive me through my young adult years and my professional career as a clinical social worker too. It embodied the already held beliefs of the Alexanders and Broesslers from whom I came.

Until this point in time my mother's working and personal life had consisted of lacklustre jobs and an inability to maintain friendships of any kind. Her relationship with her mother and sister was often estranged. She worked as a grocery store clerk, much to my chagrin and my grandfather's disappointment, as a secretary, and she never did aspire to achieve academic greatness. In fact, she was often described by her father as being mentally lazy despite a good intellect and a keen mind. I soon understood and accepted that description of her when I became an adult. She never read books though her knowledge of the classics of art and music and politics was extensive. She just said she was not interested. She never travelled and after abandoning her two other daughters when they were very young, she never sought them out again. She said she was not interested and as a child and young adult, I never pressed her for information. I think I knew that my own place in her life was tenuous and that at any moment she could again express disdain for me and I would all over again be crushed to know I was unlovable even by my mother. I had seen at first hand her cruelty and apparent disregard for my sisters. I feared she would physically leave me behind as well, as she had done when she left me with the Grays. My mother truly excelled at leaving others behind without as much as a blink of the eye.

So, it became apparent that my grandfather and not my mother was going to rescue me from my loneliness. I had hoped earlier in my life that Mama would rescue me from difficulties but she never did. I was delighted and nearly euphoric. It meant moving to a large apartment in Westwood Village, near UCLA, on the border of Beverly Hills, and attending a public high school. It meant leaving behind my friends from boarding school and living with my mother full time for the first time in my life. I had dreams of how our life together would change and my dreams could not have been more different from the reality of what happened. My mother's infantile needs continued to be front and centre as we began our life together for the first time in almost ten years. Her attempts to nurture and mother me failed miserably and as her expectations of a perfect daughter were not met, she became frustrated and more distant.

Westwood Village was created by the Janss Investment Company, run by Harold and Edwin Janss and their father, Peter, in the late 1920s as an autonomous shopping district and headquarters of the Janss Company. Its boom was complemented by the boom of UCLA (which selected the Westwood Hills as its new home in 1925), as it was developed as a shopping district not just for the residents of Westwood but also for the university. Opening in 1929, the original design was considered one of the most well planned and beautifully laid out of commercial areas in the nation. Harold Janss had hired leading architects and instructed them to follow a Mediterranean theme, with clay tile roofs, decorative Spanish tile, walkways, patios, and courtyards.

Buildings located at strategic points, including theatres, used towers to serve as beacons for drivers on Wilshire Boulevard. Janss picked the first slate of businesses and determined their location in the neighbourhood; the area opened with thirty-four businesses and, despite the Great Depression, had 452 in 1939 (Martha Groves, *LA Times*, "Seeking Shoppers in Westwood Village," May 6, 2008).

The Village was thought to be upscale economically, and in the 1950s and 1960s it housed many small and larger shops and restaurants. There were, and are still today, two major cinemas where studio premieres are often held: The Village Fox and Bruin theatres. Most of the restaurants were independently owned as were the shops with the exception of Desmonds and Bullocks, both parts of chain stores.

My life was turning upside down again but this time it would bring a major enhancement: a full time grandfather who was keenly interested in me, my school work, my friends, and my relationship with my mother. He and I both entered into our new living arrangements with hopeful confidence and the desire for better outcomes all round.

My grandfather located and rented a large three bedroom apartment/duplex at the corner of Ashton and Midvale Avenues, one block from the intersection of Westwood and Wilshire Boulevards. It was in a two-storey pink Spanish hacienda stucco building on a large corner lot. Most of the buildings in the area were single family homes, duplexes, or small apartment buildings. There were no structures taller than two storeys. The daughter of Errol Flynn lived a few blocks away and Deidre and I became firm friends soon after our moving into the neighbourhood.

The apartment was larger than anything I had lived in previously and reminded me of the La Jolla house with its wide corridors or hallways. The entry floor's black and white marble tiles were arranged in a geometric pattern and were reflected in the mirrored foyer walls. The sitting room had a wood burning fireplace with a mantle taller than me. It had a traditional floor plan with a dining room on the opposite side of the sitting room. The kitchen was big, as well, with two sinks, one of them a bar sink, and floor to ceiling cabinets where food and alcohol was stored. All the windows, and there were many, had white wood shutters. I loved those shutters and would close them at night for privacy. The bedrooms were large and one was designated as my grandfather's office where he saw patients the evenings he was in town. He would leave the hospital around 4:30 and see three patients at home before we dined together in the formal dining room. When he went to Palm Springs for the weekend to be with my grandmother, I would sleep in his bed and read the books on his bedside table, usually James Bond or Perry Mason novels. My grandfather had his own telephone, separate from the house phone, and the long cords could stretch into the kitchen. I would sit on the kitchen floor with a phone in either hand and consult with friends and make plans. Most of the furniture had come from the sale of the La Jolla house and some included hand painted items done by my grandmother. No wonder I initially felt safe and at home in this new abode.

My grandfather set about helping my mother meet more suitable and proper men as possible suitors. He hoped that perhaps potential marriage number four may be to a psychologist or physician instead of a grocery store clerk as was husband number three. He fixed her up with professional men he hoped she would be interested in and she went out on many dates, like a teenager instead of the thirty-something thrice-married woman she was. I wonder what my grandfather said to these men when describing his firstborn beautiful blonde daughter as a potential date. I would love to have been able to listen in on those conversations. I remember watching with fascination as she prepared for these romantic encounters in her new dresses from Saks Fifth Avenue, I. Magnin, or Bullocks. She appeared sophisticated and dazzling to me. I was always anxious when she left me alone. At the time I did not understand those feelings. Perhaps it was that I feared she would not return. When she left the apartment she often kissed the top of my hand and left an imprint of her ruby red lips. I would not wash my hands and would look at my hand with love throughout the night until she returned home. None of the dates resulted in a long-standing relationship and in the end my mother resented her father's interference in her social life.

At that time, during my high school years, my mother worked for an agency in Beverly Hills providing financial management services to movie stars and singers. It was the first job she obtained after leaving George number 2. Clients of the agency included Tab Hunter, Bob and his older and more successful brother, crooner Bing Crosby, and others. The office was located on Rodeo Drive, then just down the block from the Luau Restaurant and on the other side of the street. It was at this agency that my mother met Fred Dodge, a certified public accountant with the firm, who eventually left and went to work at Pickfair for Mary Pickford and Douglas Fairbanks Jr in 1960 or 1961. Like my mother, Fred was divorced, and had grown-up children who were alienated from him. He was also an alcoholic, something I did not learn until years later. My mother also began drinking to excess during those years and, coincidentally, with her fifth husband too.

Pickfair was an eighteen-acre estate in the city of Beverly Hills, California on Summit Drive, designed by architect Wallace Neff (who designed many of the homes in Rolling Hills) for silent film actors Douglas Fairbanks and Mary Pickford. Coined "Pickfair" by the press, it was one of the most celebrated homes in the world. *Life* magazine described Pickfair as "a gathering place only slightly less important than the White House … and much more fun". I grew up hearing the names of these two who were part of Hollywood royalty and thought it was amusing to hear stories that my mother would retell after she joined Fred as a member of the office staff at Pickfair. One humorous tale was that Mary Pickford would stockpile gifts from friends and colleagues and regift them long before that practice was considered socially acceptable. When my mother told me these stories I was troubled, especially when I was told that Mary Pickford often regifted to the same person the gift had originated from in the first place. Most likely she did this because of absentmindedness. I think it is sad and I am filled with pity for the woman who had been known as "America's Sweetheart".

My most difficult years of not having a loving mother figure was during puberty and high school, when it felt like everyone else had a mother but me. I was jealous because all my friends and classmates had a mother in their life. Nobody had sisters who were left behind by their mother. Nobody had a mother who did nothing with them, who preferred to spend time with her boyfriends. I was missing out and I knew it. I never expressed anger (not allowed) though I knew inside it was my fault and I alone could change it. Magical thinking played a huge part in my belief system as an adolescent.

In those years, my grandfather spent his days at Mt Sinai Hospital, overseeing his research, teaching residents and interns, and seeing patients. In the evening he came home early to see two or three patients and then we had a late dinner. He sat at the head of the long table with my mother and me on either side. We had discussions about politics, present and past, current events all around the world, music, the arts, and the daily goings on of each of us. I liked the time we all spent together; I doubt that my mother did. In fact, despite the fact that family was important to the Alexanders back in Budapest, while my grandfather was growing up, it seems this value was not believed or appreciated by my mother.

The idea of family was a concept that did not wear well with my mother. She preferred to spend time with her boyfriends or her female friends. I do not recall ever spending time with her when it was a home weekend, away from classes at Chadwick, or as a teen when we lived with Big Papa. She either passed me off upon her in-laws or her husband cared for me while she went to work. I have to say that I do not remember ever going anywhere with her, either on a shopping trip, to the movies, to an amusement park, to play tennis; I recall nothing at all. I remember only one Christmas while I was growing up, when I may have been ten or eleven years old, I remember a thirteenth birthday dinner at a pizza parlour, and then another Christmas when I was sixteen or seventeen. My mother would not be considered as one we call today a "hands on mother". Because of that, though, she inadvertently taught me important life lessons.

Since my mother did not want to spend time with me, I rationalised her behaviour as my failures. I made excuses for her. I was embarrassed by her lack of concern for me. I hardly ever invited friends to the house, preferring to go to their homes instead. I was positive that I had done something tremendously bad in order to bring about such indifference in her. I looked around at my companions and saw very different mothers and fathers. I saw caring relationships between adults and children, my friends. In fact, even as an adult, when I would describe my childhood I always thought my friends were waiting for the other shoe to drop, the missing part of the story to be told that could justify her behaviour. Like them, I thought it was my fault and that if I just tried harder to be more perfect, she would want me. But no matter how hard I tried, I always failed. She never wanted me nor did she, as years went by, want her other two daughters or her grandchildren. My mother had chosen years ago to leave us all when she chose men instead. I don't think she ever looked back or had regret of any kind until the final weeks of her life when she knew she was dying. But by then it was truly too late to make significant changes.

I had no supervision, emotional support, or company and spent most weekends with my best friend, Barbara Waxman, and her family, in Brentwood. Her father was Phil Waxman, a film producer making movies mostly for Columbia Pictures, and my mother did not approve of them. They were New Yorkers who had come to California for Barbara's father's movie business work. Barbara and I were kindred spirits. Neither of us had gone to the local junior high and knew no one in the high school when classes began. It was natural that we would fast form a friendship. Barbara's parents took me everywhere and treated me like a second daughter. I called them Aunt Ruthie and Uncle Phil and loved them dearly. They were the parents I longed for and did not have. Aunt Ruthie and Uncle Phil were good to me and took me under their wing almost each and every weekend for three years. Uncle Phil took us to the Academy Awards twice and Barbara and I went to the Academy Theater every Oscar season to view all the nominated films. They left Los Angeles most weekends and often took me with them to Palm Springs or Newport Beach and San Diego.

I do not recall that my mother ever thanked them for their care of me. In fact, my mother did not like Barbara or her parents and I thought at the time it was because they spent so much time with me whereas she spent none. She was very vocal in her dislike of Barbara. I now know, after discovering the long-held secret of my family's own Jewish heritage, that my mother was an anti-Semite and she did not approve of me hanging out with my Jewish friends. It seems ironic since most of my classmates at Chadwick were Jewish and she never said a thing to me then. I even wondered in later years if the contempt she felt for them was a cover-up of her own feelings of inadequacy as a parent. I doubt she gave a damn about that. She was concerned about their Jewishness and nothing more. Now I know she was afraid of being discovered.

My grandfather really stepped in and stepped up, and tried to be both mother and father to me. As I grew older it became normal not to have her around. It got to the point that she was gone each weekend when I was in high school and so was my grandfather. He went to Palm Springs to be with my grandmother and my mother went to Santa Monica to be with her boyfriend, the man who would become her fourth husband. She would often leave me $50 to cover expenses for the weekend. And off she went. Most times I would spend the weekend with Barbara and her family and, if not away with them, Barbara and I would take day trips and I would get home after 2 am. I was older than Barbara and could drive at the time. Barbara's parents allowed us to take their car. My mother never knew. Mama's abandonment of me, emotionally and physically, naturally led to issues later in life regarding my ability to trust others and played havoc with marital relationships as well.

It seems she mostly complained about me to her friends, about how fat I was, how embarrassed she was of me, and how I was unworkable in terms of behaviour. She certainly felt long-suffering and beleaguered because of me and I always felt I was an encumbrance to her and a reminder of responsibilities she did not want. I did what I was told, I got good grades, I neither did drugs nor smoked ... but nothing pleased her. She did not want to be around me, spend time with me, teach me anything, or share herself with me. Try as I did to get her attention and impress her, I was always unable to do so.

I felt alone even though I was living with my grandfather and my mother. I felt "over-parentified" as I was responsible for the household, the cooking, and menu planning. My mother abdicated all household responsibilities to me and my grandfather. I was even responsible for setting an alarm in order to get up earlier than her and to make sure she was up in time to get to work. In this large apartment we shared a bedroom, teenage daughter and mother. How I loathed that arrangement. Neither of us had our much-needed privacy. My grandfather paid the bills and provided financial security for my mother and me. He saw to it that I had everything I needed and everything that he thought my mother needed as well. The irony of course is that my mother did not see it that way. She was never good at expressing empathy or being aware of others' activities and motivations. She was always just about herself.

My grandfather's colleagues at the hospital knew and saw my unhappiness. They sensed that everything was not OK at home and tried to intervene. I was referred to a clinical psychologist, for what, I do not really know. I interpreted it at the time that I was being sent because I was bad. I felt bad. Like I felt bad when I was sent away to Chadwick. My mother did not want me near her nor did she like me. I took the bus to the appointment and my mother never accompanied me nor did we discuss the sessions. I went on my own. I remember taking both an IQ test and a Rorschach test (I was told my IQ was 139). I do not recall how many appointments there were, but it was most certainly not a long relationship. These appointments did not bring about the desired result and I continued to feel estranged and alone. The rift between my mother and me reached an impasse one day in the kitchen. The incident turned out to be a turning point for all of us though I would only learn that later on. I did not know it at the time.

My friend Barbara was visiting me and Mama and I were having a disagreement about something, most likely something entirely trivial. Mama was reprimanding me in front of my friend and I politely asked her to scold me later when my friend was no longer present. My mother refused to stop berating me, her voice becoming louder. When I did not stop talking, she slapped me and I impulsively slapped her back. She began to scream and, all of a sudden, Big Papa, who was with a patient in his study, came down the hall into the kitchen and sternly scolded my mother, "Can't you keep the child quiet?" I can still see his coat tails extended out from his body as he swiftly navigated the short distance from the den to the kitchen down the narrow hallway. It seemed to me as if he had merely floated into the kitchen though his mood was very angry.

After this incident I think that my grandfather grew more critical and vocal of my mother's parenting style. He began to again take a more active role in the decisions regarding my well-being. I do not think my mother liked whatever suggestions he may have had for her nor did she like the criticism. Her fragile self could not tolerate such censure from her own father and, hence, she needed to find a way out of the living arrangement, however fortuitous it may have appeared initially. She wanted to be left alone and she needed to end whatever scrutiny she perceived as coming from my grandfather. Mostly she wanted to make whatever decision she wished without interference. It's kind of immature really; the desire to not be responsible or accountable.

Later that year, when it was time for the new school year to begin, my mother informed me that we would no longer be living with my grandfather. We would seek and find a smaller apartment in the same school district so that I could finish high school with my friends though there was a brief discussion about attending Catholic school where the nuns would better control me. We moved less than five or six blocks away and, as an impressionable teen, I was mortified when I saw our much smaller accommodations. I was embarrassed and humiliated. My friends were wealthy. I was accustomed to living a lifestyle similar to theirs. It was clear to me that my mother was now our sole support.

The apartment she chose was on Veteran Avenue near Santa Monica Boulevard in Westwood. It was so small that I had the only bedroom; with my own television. She slept on a sofa bed in the sitting room and spent most weekends with her boyfriend in Santa Monica. I dreamed of applying to colleges although she made it clear she would not help me financially and she was not particularly supportive of the idea. She thought I should just get married, like her. It was at that moment I first began to fully comprehend that I was going to be on my own from then on. I had just turned seventeen and I was a senior in high school.

I had dinner with Big Papa at least once a week. He encouraged me to speak German with him and we had fun together. He treated me to my favourite desserts, a chocolate éclair or a Napoleon, and I looked forward to our time together. He disliked eating dinner alone and since the break-up, liked to spoil me. Our getting together weekly was just the right medicine for both of us. I tried to fill my weekends with time away from home and studied when Mama was home. We spent no time together.

I graduated from high school in mid-June 1962. That day I came home from dinner at one of the restaurants on La Cienega Boulevard, with my mother and her boyfriend, to find flowers at the door. The flowers were from my father with a note congratulating me on the high school graduation. This was the first time I had ever heard from my father. He had just been given a position as a nuclear physicist with the Atomic Energy Commission in Washington DC and, as part of the employment process, the FBI contacted my grandfather and my mother for background checks and a security clearance. My grandfather contacted my father and informed him that I was graduating from high school soon. My father decided to send flowers and that was my entrée into my father's world and his into mine.

A few days later my mother went to Reno and married her boyfriend, Fred Dodge. She returned to our apartment and informed me that she was moving to Nevada. I was confused. I did not want to go to Nevada. I wanted to go to college in LA where I had grown up and where I had friends and family. My grandfather continued to spend at least four days at the hospital each week. I wanted to be close to him. My mother said that either I was to go with her or she would leave me behind. She told me not to call her. She told me never to contact her by phone collect. She left two days later. I was essentially homeless and without the means to support myself.

Overnight I had become an emancipated minor without my intent. Mama up and left me, as easy as she had left her other

61

two children years before. Any thought that I may have had that she cared for me immediately evaporated; vanished in thin air, just like she did. I was filled with rage and contempt for her. Those feelings would continue for many years and disrupt many relationships.

My grandfather rescued me again and offered me a position typing a manuscript he was working on: *The History of Psychiatry*. I typed for him and he paid me $5/hour. Someone arranged, I do not know who, that I would live in a boarding house in downtown Los Angeles run by the Sisters of Social Service. Since it was a Catholic-run home I think the family thought it was a good arrangement. I was there less than two months when I found myself living with my newly married aunt and uncle in the Pacific Palisades. I really do not know how this all happened. I think my grandfather was concerned about outward appearances. It did not look good for his granddaughter to be living in a residence for homeless girls. He must have paid my aunt to take me in and I was grateful. I knew nothing of the particulars, do not know them today either, but can surmise what may have occurred.

By installing me in the home of my aunt, a social psychologist and researcher with a keen mind, whose friends were of similar character, Big Papa continued to set the stage for my later development to become an independent thinker and one who contributes to society. If I had moved to Nevada with my mother, this would not have happened.

I moved in with my aunt and uncle sometime during the summer of 1962. Although my mother was again absolved of her parenting responsibilities, she was none too happy that her younger sister had stepped into her shoes. At the time I was filled with anger. I hated her. I hated her for leaving me. I hated her for not loving me. I often thought I wished I were older, I wished I were a mother, I wished I could bestow on my own child the love I did not receive from my own mother. I was miserable and remained angry for a very long time. Even though I had a home with my aunt and uncle, I was lost. Totally lost and on my own. Again. I was just about to turn eighteen.

My aunt and uncle lived in the Pacific Palisades, a small affluent coastal community between Santa Monica and Malibu and bordered on the east by Brentwood. When Kiki left Chicago a few years before, she settled into a small guest cottage just north of Sunset Boulevard and preferred to remain in the area after she and Jack married. The Palisades, as it is known locally, is a small town and is part of Los Angeles proper. It was founded in the 1920s by the Reverend Charles H. Scott and the Southern California Methodist Episcopal Church when they bought land and pictured an elaborate religious-intellectual commune. Believers snapped up choice lots and lived in tents during construction. In one subdivision, streets were named for Methodist missionaries. The tents eventually were replaced by cabins, then by bungalows, and ultimately by multimillion-dollar homes. Interestingly, for many decades there was a virtual ban on drinking alcohol in the area, and a local Chinese restaurant, House of Lee, held the only liquor licence. This ban no doubt was a holdover from the community's religious beginnings.

Jack and Kiki lived in a newly built contemporary home overlooking Temescal Canyon on Muskingum Drive. The furnishings were modern and there was a lot of teak in the home. The TV was kept in the cupboard in the sitting room and there was no phone in that room, either. This was a custom I knew as a youngster and to this day, there is neither a phone nor a TV in my sitting room. To the left of the house was the ocean and to the right Sunset Boulevard. The neighbourhood was young and most families had small children. As a student in the local junior college, I often babysat for the neighbourhood children. Kiki was completing a PhD in social psychology at the University of Southern California and Jack was a probation officer for the county of Los Angeles and was away from the home every other week, at a residential home for delinquent boys, in the Malibu Hills.

Kiki soon secured a position as a professor at one of the state universities and I eventually transferred to this school as a junior. At that time Jack worked downtown and we dropped him off and continued to the campus further along. I found a part-time job as a clerk/typist for two professors in the Pupil Personnel and Guidance Department, Dr Jane Matson and Dr David Bilovsky. It was perfect. I could work in-between classes and earn a little bit of money. It seemed idyllic and as if it was meant to be. I formed an almost immediate attachment to both of these psychologists, but most of all to Dr Matson who would become my second surrogate mother. She, unlike my aunt, would never be a disappointment to me nor would she ever abandon me.

I nicknamed Dr Jane Matson "Dr M" as it was an affectionate term that also showed respect. It implied closeness and intimacy. It seemed the best of both worlds. She was a single professional woman who had lost the love of her life during World War II. She never married and had no children. I became the daughter she never had and she became the mother I never had. She was loving and kind, she was generous and supportive. She was reliable and consistent. She was never cross with me though she let me know when she disapproved of my actions from time to time. She certainly did not approve of the way my aunt, mother, and grandmother would disown me after my grandfather's death and she often spoke to my aunt, her colleague, about me and how she thought the family should care for me. But, first we must return to the aftermath of Big Papa's death and how it left me searching for another father figure.

Westwood Village in the late 1950s.

Ilonka's 9th grade school picture.

1011 Cielo Drive in Palm Springs. The winter home of Ilonka's grandparents where she spent a lot of time. The house has been placed on the Register of US Historical Properties and is a prime example of mid century modern architecture having been designed by Walter S. White.

CHAPTER FIVE

The fear of failure, again

On an early and bright Sunday morning in March 1964, while living with my aunt and uncle, Kiki and Jack, I heard the phone ring. It was before 7 am. The call came from my grandmother in Palm Springs to tell us that my beloved grandfather, Big Papa, had just died. I remember dressing hastily and climbing into the back of my aunt's VW bug to travel the 100 miles to The Springs. Kiki ran every red light and stop sign in order to make good time. I do not recall if there was conversation during the trip and I do not recall a discussion about what would happen next.

Although I was at the time nineteen, a college student, and in some cultures nineteen is considered an adult, I was treated like a child by my family. I was never included in considerations concerning my future or anything else significant regarding other family members. When we arrived in Palm Springs my aunt informed me that my grandmother "was too upset for me to come to the house" and therefore I would need to stay in a hotel, alone, until the funeral a few days later. When I begged, through tears, not to be left alone, I was silenced with money, as was often the case, and told to be a good girl. Hell, I was always a good girl: I did what I was told, I did not answer back to parents or adults, and I studied hard and attained good grades. I do not know who made the decision to sequester me away in a hotel while the family gathered at the house or when the decision was made. At the time it never occurred to me to question the edict though I wish now, years later, that I had been more assertive. I was taught to keep my mouth closed in the company of adults. I was literally taught to not speak until spoken to and acknowledged. I almost always did what I was told. I feared rejection if I did not do what was expected of me.

Those two or three days were interminable and are now a total fog. I do not know the name of the hotel, however I do know it was on Palm Canyon Drive. I do not know how I passed the days, if and where I ate, or how I coped through all the tears and fearfulness of being left alone, abandoned yet again. By this time I had not seen my mother in three years and I knew she was at the house. She never asked to see me; she did not call, and never expressed any interest or concern in anyone other than herself.

At long last I was liberated from the enforced solitude, so to speak, on the day of the funeral. I do not know who came to pick me up to take me to the Catholic church, but someone did. I was not allowed to sit with the family and close friends that included my mother, my aunt, and my grandmother. I sat in the first pew with my aunt's surrogate mother, Dr Hedda Bolgar, a colleague of my grandfather who had followed him to Los Angeles from Chicago, and her husband Herbie. Hedda and Herbie had befriended me after I came to live with Kiki and Jack and I spent most holidays in their home a few blocks from the beach in Santa Monica. I remember that the spring heat of Palm Springs mixed with the many flowers in the crowded church made for a most unpleasant odour. It was noxious and sweet and challenging to endure. Neither my mother nor my grandmother spoke to me at the church.

Hedda and Herbie drove me to the house at 1011 Cielo Drive in the Tuscany Hills suburb of Palm Springs. The house is a modern edifice erected ten years earlier under the watchful eye of my grandmother and architect Walter S. White. I was wearing a black silk shirtdress from Saks Fifth Avenue and my face was streaked from crying. I held on to the hand of Hedda as I entered the filled room. My grandmother pointed at me and asked, "Who is that?" The room grew silent until Pauline Phillips, better known as Dear Abby, an old family friend, said, "Annie that is Ilonka." My grandmother's response was, "Get her out of here, she looks awful." Neither my mother nor my aunt came to my rescue and I was hurriedly removed from the house and went back to the hotel, alone, to cope with my anguish and palpable grief.

It was incredible to me then, as it is now, that my family would treat me in this way, would treat anyone in this way, at such a difficult and vulnerable time. I internalised their behaviour and blamed myself though I did not know what I had done. I just believed that I was bad and had obviously done something horrendous in order to be treated in such a manner, before the world's foremost analysts and psychiatrists. I knew I was a colossal disappointment to the three most important people in my life who were, coincidentally, all women: my mother, my grandmother, and my aunt. At that time I did not have a clinical social work education. I had not yet studied psychopathology and psychological disorders, and in particular, personality disorders. It would be years before I would learn that the women in my life were broken and therefore their responses to me were not normal. It was not my fault. I had done nothing wrong. But that lesson and its resultant compassion for their wounding behaviour and criticism towards me did not come for decades.

I realised at that precise moment, the day of my grandfather's funeral, that I was totally and unequivocally alone. I had lost my grandfather but also lost my father figure and the one person who was always an advocate for me. He was my friend and confidant. From here on, I would be on my own. Alone, again. My mother had left me three years before after a lifetime of being distant emotionally, when she moved to Reno with her fourth husband. Now my grandfather had left me and there was no one. I had absolutely no one to trust. Oh, I was still living with my mother's younger sister and her husband, but the writing was on the wall and I knew my time with them, in a somewhat normal household, was limited. I had been taken in to placate my grandfather's fear of a potentially tarnished reputation and I would soon have to be put out of that home, too. His death released my aunt from any obligation she may have felt to help her father, my grandfather, and me. I learned soon thereafter that my aunt and uncle were trying to have a baby and I was, therefore, not needed anymore as their make-believe daughter when a true son was to be born a couple of years later.

When we returned home from the funeral in Palm Springs to the Palisades, I returned to my college classes. My aunt and uncle returned to work and plans were made for a Los Angeles based memorial honouring my grandfather the following weekend. I do not remember where it was held; somewhere in Santa Monica, but either on the drive home, or at the memorial, my uncle Jack suffered a heart attack. He was admitted to St John's Hospital in Santa Monica and a day later my father contacted me and informed me he was in California and wanted to come by and meet me. What an avalanche of emotions. My immediate reaction was, "Why are you here and not my Big Papa? He is the one I want, not you." At least I had the proper rearing to refrain from saying that to him when we met a few days later, though it was front and centre in my mind and heart. Imagine. Losing your only father figure and meeting your biological father for the first time in fewer than ten days' time. It can only be described as momentous and yet apocalyptic.

I was angry that my grandfather died and left me alone and that my father was alive. I was angry that my father had never wanted to see me before, or so I thought at the time, and wondered why would he suddenly want to see me, now? I did not believe him and I was suspicious of everything he said and his motives. It was not until years later that I learned my grandfather had made an attempt to bribe my father with $50,000 when I was a toddler to stay away and allow my mother to remarry and permit her second husband to adopt me. My father told me that he refused the money but agreed to stay away because, "He was Dr Alexander. He knew what was best for you. I trusted him." My grandfather convinced my father to relinquish his parental rights. (My father would often say to me, "But I am not your legal father," as if justification for his total lack of involvement or assistance in my life prior to his arrival when I was nineteen.)

As it turned out, my father learned of my grandfather's death and waited until then to make an entrance into my life as he had made that promise years before. Instead of being a monster, he was a man of honour. He was honouring a pledge made, albeit a misguided promise, to a man who he and the world considered great and powerful. A promise that was extracted by someone who most certainly knew better. The decision my grandfather made to exclude my father from my life may just be his most misguided decision. But, with regard to decisions made that altered my life and my mother's life, there were many other mistakes with resultant negative consequences for all that were made by the all-knowing and powerful Franz Alexander.

My father and I began to learn about each other. He took me to his parents' home in Encino which was about a twenty minute drive from where I had grown up in Beverly Hills and Westwood Village. I had no idea they were so geographically close by and I am sure my mother did not know that either. At least it was never mentioned in front of me. All I knew was that my father was known in the Alexander family circles as George number 1. I did not know his complete name until I was in high school. I did not learn that my mother's second husband, the man who adopted me, was not my biological father until

I was in the third or fourth grade. I was dumbfounded and only was told I was adopted. I had no real clear understanding of what it meant except I was again with my mother, and my two half-sisters were with who I would start to call, in my adult life, "my Thomas father". It was confusing and I was an unhappy little girl.

When my father drove me from the home I shared with my aunt and uncle to his parents' home in the San Fernando Valley, I remember being fearful and panicky. Those feelings soon left me. I was met by loving and accepting grandparents, an aunt and uncle and cousins, and felt immediately at home. I recalled in later life how contradictory it all was. My grandparents, my Big Mama and Big Papa, and my mother, looked down on the Rotariu branch of the family as being beneath them and not good enough. How ironic that it was this arm of the family that would show me unconditional love and acceptance. This arm that would help me financially and emotionally when my Alexander family would not. This arm that would help me learn the important lesson of focusing on what you have instead of longing for what can never be. This arm of the family that would be my rock in young adulthood and throughout the rest of my life. This arm of the family would teach me how to love and how to be loved. Close cousins would show me just how a sibling relationship should be as they took me in and made a sister of me.

I grew up as an only child. I had no relatives other than my mother, my aunt, and my grandparents. To be able to share feelings and characteristics with cousins, who shared some of the same traits with me, was eye-opening for me. I had felt totally alone and was desperate for company. I was taught that attention was given only when excellence was achieved, and not before. I was taught that one's time was often spent on achieving and learning with the end goal being excellence. With excellence came admiration and love. Or so I thought. I did know that everyday love was something that never came to me from my mother. She neither appreciated nor wanted a child in her life. What I never understood, however, is that when my mother walked away from her two other children, these two girls were never accepted as grandchildren by Big Papa. They were never seen again. That is why although I had two sisters I always considered myself an only child.

My paternal grandparents hugged and kissed me. When my name was changed my grandparents were never informed. At our initial meeting, my grandmother Anna brought out a lovely portrait of me that was sent to her by my mother when I was about a year or eighteen months old, when my mother divorced their son. This was the only tangible reminder of a granddaughter Nina who had been taken from their lives. Now they had to accept that I was no longer Nina, in fact I never knew about the name until years later, but I understand how difficult it must have been for them. Immediately after they welcomed me in person, they relinquished the photo to me, and I have it still. It was an affectionate moment and I will remember it all the days of my life.

My paternal grandparents left Chicago after their daughter, Vicki, married and moved to California with her new husband at the end of World War II. Vicki was born almost four years after my father and was the apple of her mother's eye. Mother and daughter lived in the same small town of Encino and were totally immersed in each other's lives without being intrusive. But I digress.

In retrospect it is clear to me that my aunt and uncle, Kiki and Jack, did not feel obligated to continue providing a home for me after Big Papa died in 1964. I finished the school year at their home and the following year was encouraged or told to find a housing arrangement with friends closer to my own age. Again I interpreted this, at the time, as their disapproval and internalised my familiar feelings of being bad and not good enough. I felt as though my attempt to be their imaginary daughter had been a failure. I knew all too well what failure felt like.

I wore not being good enough as a comfortable overcoat. By the time I was twenty, I had been abandoned by my mother and by my first surrogate mother, my own mother's sister, my aunt. I had earlier been abandoned by my grandmother at the time of my grandfather's death. I was alone and thought I had no other Alexander relatives.

During my teen years, while living with my mother, I often spent summer days at the beach in Santa Monica. I would ride the number 83 green MTA bus along Wilshire Boulevard and get off at the Fourth Street Overpass and walk down the ramp to the beach below and meet my girlfriend. While camping out at the same lifeguard station each day, and meeting regulars at the beach, I made an acquaintance with a much older man. At that time I was interested in political science and hoped to study the law. This man was a Beverly Hills lawyer who lived in the Pacific Palisades. His son was a lifeguard and he often walked the beach after his legal workday ended. He had a house near the beach and knew all the regulars and all the lifeguards.

Dan Schnabel grew up in Fresno and attended Stanford University where he graduated Phi Beta Kappa. He then attended USC Law School and Georgetown Medical School. When the Second World War broke out he enlisted in the US Navy and was trained as a pilot. After the war was over, he opened up a law practice in Beverly Hills and his first major case was to represent Kay Spreckels in her divorce from Clark Gable in the early 1950s. Dan was tall, blond, worldly, intelligent, and interested in my girlfriend Kildae Carroll and me. He encouraged me to attend law school and he thought I had a keen mind. He paid me attention where my mother did not.

After I moved from the Palisades to be closer to school and left the home of my aunt and uncle, I lost track of my friend Dan. A year or two went by and we reconnected. He often came to take me to dinner and to listen to my woes and my dreams. He helped me obtain financial scholarships and when

I was drifting and did not know where to turn for assistance and guidance, he along with Dr M helped me chart my course. I then "fell under the spell" of this much older man who provided security, kindness, and direction for the first time since my grandfather died. I studied jurisprudence and constitutional history, no doubt to ensure that I would continue to curry his favour. I most likely knew he was meeting some of my needs for parental involvement and was fearful I could lose him too, as I had lost my grandfather and my father before him.

During these years, my aunt and uncle welcomed a son (Alex Levine) and had nothing to do with me. It was as if I no longer existed. (I see in retrospect that Kiki was doing what my mother and grandparents had done before when my mother walked away from me emotionally and physically and when my mother left her two small children and my grandparents never to acknowledge them again.) I did not know then that they disapproved of my relationship with Dan but I think their decision to walk away from me was partly because I was beginning to think for myself and no longer felt the need to express adoration for Kiki. I was no longer meeting her needs in terms of reflecting back her brilliance or how wonderful I thought she was or how I was nothing without her. I now understand her narcissistic needs and that I was no longer willing to disempower myself in order to please her.

Eventually my relationship with Dan became a sexual one. We often travelled together and he took me to Europe three times, we went to many of the islands in the Caribbean including Puerto Rico and Jamaica, and we went to South America and all through Mexico. He also guided me through my most difficult years in college. Years when I spent more time drinking and hanging out with friends than at class. Years when I protested and marched and picketed and became involved in many student demonstrations for civil rights, against the war in Vietnam, and belonged to most student groups such as SNCC and NAACP. I often boarded a bus on Friday at UCLA in order to go to Berkeley to attend such demonstrations. Dan's insight helped me learn why I was attracted to these organisations and how it was related to what I had learned about helping others from my grandfather. Dan became the single most important male in my life after my grandfather's death.

I know now that Dan was meeting my needs for stability and security. I did not have this from my family and was in dire need of it. He recognised my needs and was able to meet them for several years until I was able to stand on my own two feet. He saw something special in me and I believe he was like my grandfather in that way. Because of this relationship, my aunt and uncle turned their backs on me once again. I never spoke to them after 1967 or 1968 until Christmas 1993 when I was summoned to come to their home to learn of Kiki's breast cancer diagnosis. Even upon learning of this illness, our estrangement did not mend. I never saw my aunt again. She died of breast cancer in the fall of 1994. That is one funeral I did attend though my mother refused to leave Reno and go with me: "I don't do funerals." My father's younger sister, my aunt Vicki, said, "I will go to the funeral with you. I will not let you experience that alone."

As the years have gone by I have never felt ashamed or embarrassed by my relationship with Dan. It is from him that I began to learn that men and fathers can be reliable, trustworthy, and kind. I was fortunate to have him rescue me when I needed help. I am grateful for the lessons he taught me about life, myself, the world, and the importance of helping others. I know that he and my grandfather would have been friends and not foes as they did share many of the same attributes and core values.

My fear of failure and the consequence of poor choices caused me to fritter away my twenties and thirties. I married one of the first men who showed interest in me after Dan told me, "You must marry someone your own age." I married an actor from Ontario, Canada who was studying at the Pasadena

Playhouse in Southern California. We set up house in Pasadena and I applied for and obtained positions as an actuarial assistant at two major life insurance companies. Darryl wanted to move to Europe to see if his dream of achieving success as an actor might be realised faster in Italy. We moved to Rome in the autumn of 1970 and success did not come fast enough for either of us. After we returned home to California, he began a series of liaisons with other women, one of whom became pregnant, and we separated in the summer of 1973 and divorced not long thereafter.

Almost impulsively I contacted one of Darryl's friends in Toronto, a man I had met while on vacation, and made arrangements to spend part of Christmas with him, and to visit my father in the DC area afterwards. During that quick trip to Toronto I met and slept with a man (What was I thinking? Most likely I was not thinking.) who would become husband number 2, Tom. I returned to Los Angeles after my Christmas holidays and began to make immediate plans to immigrate to Canada which I did in the spring of 1974. Tom and I married in November 1974 in a small church in northern Ontario about 100 miles north of Toronto. I began to work for the director of the dialysis unit at the University of Toronto Hospital and seemed to have found my stride. I liked my work and I enjoyed meeting interesting people, some of whom were draft dodgers now in a Canadian medical school. I went to the University of Toronto and asked to apply to medical school. The clerk in the admissions office told me I was too old. I was twenty-nine. Of course my compliant self just accepted this statement and I did not challenge her. At the time I had no idea I was making poor choices. Poor choices most likely made as I was alone with no family to support, guide, or encourage me.

In 1977 Tom and I moved to Los Angeles in order for him to complete undergraduate university and obtain a master's degree in literature. His ambitions always included writing novels and he is an extremely driven and smart man.

Unfortunately our temperaments and needs were divergent and the marriage broke down in year seven or eight. We divorced officially sometime in 1981. We continue to be friends and his nieces and nephews still call me auntie. His brother insists that, "You divorced Tom; you did not divorce his family."

Children do not grow up in a vacuum and although I was sequestered away from family in a boarding school, my family played an all-important role in my upbringing. Parents and families influence us either directly or indirectly. The Alexanders directly (and indirectly while I was living at Chadwick) taught me the importance of societal values. This included learning the difference between right and wrong, the importance of a religious education (though it was Catholic and not our Jewish heritage), teaching about how to interact with people, and life's basic rules and expectations. Indirectly parents can indoctrinate and socialise their children by example. I know it's a harsh thing to say, but I mostly learnt how not to behave from observing my parents' and my grandparents' behaviour. I figured out early that their take on the world was, to say the least, somewhat skewed and not really how I wanted to be. I learned from my parents that men are unreliable and not to be trusted. Sadly, I didn't get closer to my father when we at last met. He was just not very good at opening up. I learned the importance of being self-sufficient and independent from my mother who was neither. I learned that relationships do not always endure. I learned these lessons as I watched my mother interact with others and as I came to grips with abandonment by her and by not one, but two fathers. I think it is entirely possible to form one's own values, standards, and outlook, and to then separate from your family. All of this impacted how I developed my own moral self as I began to make decisions and choices for myself in later life.

I grew up with no confidence. If you firmly believe that your own mother doesn't love you, and your father left you as an infant, why should anyone else like you? And even at the age of seven, when I was trundled off to boarding school, I knew this wasn't something most mothers did. While, of course, many fathers walk out on their families, it's still most unusual for a mother to leave a marriage without wanting custody of her children, let alone go on to have little or no contact with them. But that is what my mother did when she left my step-father, my two sisters, and it continued to impact me for a very long time.

During these years I had no contact with my mother. I always informed my mother of what was going on in my life and hoped for a birthday or a Christmas card. I received nothing. She showed no interest in me whatsoever. I wonder why I expected something different than her usual modus operandi. Once back in California, with Tom, I wrote to my mother and she answered me. This was most likely in 1978 or 1979. Almost fifteen years had transpired since I last saw her at Big Papa's funeral in Palm Springs. Tom and I then spent a week with my mother and her husband in Reno. They all played golf together. It was awkward and felt unnatural. I had by then developed a circumspect way of viewing my mother and knew she could not express warmth to me. I think we even returned to Reno that year to spend the Christmas holidays with them.

I lost my mother so young which led to my growing up too fast and taking on more responsibility than was age appropriate. While I was capable and wanted to be fiercely independent and self-sufficient, I always found it difficult to adapt to new situations. For this reason, I am prone to demand sameness in my home and a near impossible standard for neatness. It is as if this was the only thing I could control as a child and that need carries over in my adulthood.

I think that part of my mother's emotional legacy, albeit her teaching to me, is that I can throw myself into relationships too quickly, something that is most likely a result of Mama's abandonment or her frequent change of husbands. I learned from her that men are unreliable and they eventually leave. I learned the importance of self-reliance though my mother never achieved this until her seventh decade in life (the only time she lived alone without a husband). It seems that I have always been searching for a secure family unit that I didn't have as a child. The need to belong is one that never leaves us regardless of solid friendships, career success, or financial success.

I eventually learned and accepted, with the help of surrogate mothers and psychotherapy, that my mother's emotional and physical rejection of me had more to do with her inadequacies than my faults. I learned and accepted that my father's decision to walk away was to please my grandfather who he thought knew best. I learned and accepted that my grandfather's request that my father allow another man to adopt me was motivated by his desire that his own daughter's choice of husband would create a stable home for me. It is with compassion and forgiveness that I say these things now. But I would be lying and hiding my feelings if I said that rejection and abandonment does not sometimes rule me and my emotions. In the darkest of times, when I feel alone and scared, I remember the feelings I had as a child. Sometimes these feelings overwhelm me and I suddenly find tears streaming down my face. It is as if I become that child again, scared and helpless. I am, however, able to steel myself and realise I am neither helpless nor a child now. I remember feeling not good enough, no matter what I achieved. I remember that there must have been something really wrong if your own mother and father do not want you.

I believe we each have one or two issues that we carry throughout our lives and that at each of our life's challenges, these reappear but in decreasing intensity. That is my belief and my experience. The challenge for me has always been to continue to strive for internal peace and acceptance of the past and, as the Serenity Prayer says, to accept what we cannot change. I set about changing me.

CHAPTER SIX

Big Papa to the rescue again

During my social work schooling my grandmother died. This was another funeral that I was not allowed to attend, and to make sure, my aunt and mother told me of her death after the burial had taken place in Santa Monica in November of 1984. I was in my second year of social work school at USC. This brought about questions as to why the important women in my life could be so insensitive and cruel. Not long after the funeral I received a phone call from none other than Hedda, the analyst who had followed Big Papa to LA from Chicago. She had been a friend and confidante when I lived with Kiki during my college years.

From Hedda I learned these women, my grandmother and my aunt and my mother to a lesser degree, all suffered from borderline personality disorder. I knew enough then to recognise that this poor coping strategy is often passed on in families. I wondered why I had not embraced these coping mechanisms myself. My grandfather's colleague told me at the time, "You were away at school. You were not raised by these women. You were saved. You are stronger. Kiki has a borderline personality disorder but I love her anyway." Despite the encouraging words from a well-respected psychoanalyst, I still felt alone, not good enough, and somehow bad because I was excluded from Big Mama's funeral. The unanswered questions from long ago began to haunt me again: how could this level of pain and psychological abuse occur in *this* family? How could this happen in my family, a family of highly educated psychologists and analysts? In Big Papa's family? I was not to learn the truth for many years and I would remain perplexed until the secrets were uncovered.

After years of working in academic medicine, learning a lot about haemodialysis, bladder and testicular cancer, and death and dying issues, I decided to continue my formal education. I was at the time engaged to marry a urology surgical medical trainee at USC who had attended the Air Force Academy as an undergraduate before attending medical school at Georgetown University in Washington, DC. Because Michael was still technically on active duty with the Air Force, he could possibly be required to spend time wherever the Air Force thought necessary upon completion of his training, which was three years off. My plans to obtain a doctorate in psychology could, then, most likely not be completed at one university. Since I wanted to become a therapist and not a researcher, after consultation with friends (former colleagues of my grandfather) who were social workers, and my former undergraduate surrogate mother and a clinical psychologist, Dr M, I decided to apply to graduate school and pursue a master's degree in social work instead. That course of study was a two year programme and I knew I could finish it at the same institution before Michael might be assigned to another hospital. (As it turned out, I did not have to consider these issues because soon the engagement broke off and the relationship ended.)

I looked at the two major universities in Southern California, cross town rivals, USC and UCLA, and decided on the former. Though I had attended classes and worked at UCLA, I was then working at USC and it seemed the most obvious choice. I never truly considered UCLA and did not apply there. My aunt had achieved her doctorate in social psychology at USC years before and I knew that my grandfather had a connection to USC's medical school as well. I completed the mandatory application and wrote an essay about why I was choosing clinical social work and what were my career goals and ambitions. By that time I had come to the conclusion that it was almost destiny that I follow in the footsteps of the most important person in my life: my Big Papa. Though dead now more than twenty years, his influence on my decision making still was strong as also was my need to make him proud. Having only received praise and recognition from him during my life, the psychic requirement for approval seemed to be never ending nor fulfilled.

I also believed that the timing was right and that it had not been before this. It was time for me to embark on this personal and professional journey and take control of my life as I had never been able to do previously. I felt for such a long time that I was always on the sea, rudderless and adrift. Now, after making the decision to attend social work school, I felt buoyed and full of anticipation and eagerness as I finally accepted what I thought was my fate as the granddaughter of Franz Alexander. I learned while working at UCLA and USC that I had a good mind, that I was smart and dedicated to learning, and that I had potential to be a leader. After I sent off the application to USC, I was a little fretful as some of my undergraduate grades were not as good as they should have been. I had spent a lot of time in college protesting the war in Vietnam and attending sit-ins on campus, and not as much time as I should attending class and studying diligently.

I did not know at the time that my grandfather's lifelong dream was to integrate psychoanalysis into a medical school or that this dream had been actualised at USC just prior to his death twenty years before. In retrospect I believe I was destined to attend USC and those feelings or inclination may explain why I elected to apply only there.

To my surprise, and never-ending gratitude, USC accepted me right away. I thought for many years that I was accepted because of my psychoanalytic nobility status, that is, because

I was the granddaughter of the famous Franz Alexander and it would be a feather in the cap of the dean of the School of Social Work to say this to other USC administrators. Perhaps I was accepted because USC had established the Franz Alexander Chair in Psychoanalysis in the School of Medicine in the 1960s, but I either did not remember, know, or understand that implication and/or connection. Be that as it may, I will never know. In the end, once accepted into the MSW programme, I still had to execute and do well as a member of the class of 1985.

I remember with clear recall the first day of class in September of 1983. I remember where I sat in the auditorium, who I reached out to in order to make friends, and what I wore that day. I was on my own, alone, and without much backing. I had no family to help me financially and I borrowed money to attend graduate school. I walked into the first day of Orientation, looked around at the 100 other people in our class, and wondered, "What are you doing here, what are you trying to prove?" A third of my class had the fresh-scrubbed faces of those just graduated from undergraduate school and another third were people like me, in their thirties, seeking a change. The final third were adults at the end of their working life, in their fifties or sixties, who had decided to recommit to another profession. I remember thinking positively about USC and its decision to include those older folks in our class. I was impressed and happy to be at USC. I knew then I had made a good decision and some of my anxiety and trepidation about performance left me.

My days at USC were fun, productive, and important to me. I discovered that I was still capable of learning at "this late age" and that I could achieve stellar marks. My first year placement was at a community mental health clinic run by the Los Angeles County Department of Mental Health. This office was located in Bellflower, California and was close to the Metropolitan State Hospital in Norwalk, California which housed chronic schizophrenics at the time. My placement of choice had a long training relationship with USC and three or four recent MSW graduates were on the staff in the outpatient clinic. My supervisor was an experienced and kind woman who provided a nurturing place for my learning. I was placed with another woman, older than me, who had more lived experience than me and who had been working in a group home for several years. I really looked up to her, admired her strong sense of self, and her common sense. Unfortunately it soon became apparent as we discussed course materials and expectations of different professors that this woman had poor writing skills and could not perform up to the standards of USC. (I later found out she had someone else write her entrance essay.) Sometime during the start of our second term she was placed on academic probation and ultimately left the programme. She was an African American and blamed me and my whiteness and my grandfather for her failure, and said too much was expected of her because of me. I was hurt and confused. No such thing had happened. It was upsetting to finish the school year without her at my side sharing our office. Though I am Franz Alexander's granddaughter, at that time I really knew nothing of his significant contributions to the field of American psychoanalysis and psychosomatic medicine. For her to blame her problems on my famous grandfather was juvenile and irresponsible. I know that now but that did not help me at the time when I felt confusion and sadness. I finished the year's placement and my academics with all A grades.

The younger fellow students eagerly and enthusiastically started to form a study group and made it clear they wanted me to join them. Because I earned all As during my first year of social work school, I was awarded a scholarship from the American Cancer Society for my second year and also was eligible for a stipend from the Veterans Administration when I accepted a placement at a local hospital as a social work intern working with head and neck cancer patients. The years at USC and UCLA, surrounded by cancer patients, and the four years earlier working with kidney patients on dialysis in

Canada, showed me that working with dying cancer patients never proved too much for me. I had spent more than ten years working in academic medicine, getting to know the patients in the office, and knew how to offer support and how to listen. I immersed myself in Yalom's group techniques and Kubler-Ross's stages of death and dying as I prepared for my second year's field placement on a head and neck cancer ward.

I had already learned the importance of adequate or good enough mothering ten or more years before. I learned that other women could take the place of what my mother was unable to do for me. I had already had one such replacement mother, Dr M, the psychologist for whom I worked for a year or two as an undergraduate student. She was an expert in the junior college counselling movement and each summer session hosted counsellors from across the country in a teaching institute. I was often asked to be a volunteer patient for the newly trained to try out their skills. Dr M and her guidance, love, and attention provided the nurturance and stability so important to me during my early twenties after my grandfather died and my aunt and mother abandoned me. Even as I write this, as a host mother to international students, I wonder, who abandons their own child? It is impossible for me to understand.

During my second year of social work school, aside from learning how to become an effective therapist, I learned it was OK to begin to trust the other women who came into my life. I already had Dr M as a lifelong friend, and now I had the good fortune to meet Emma Barcelona Caparros, my supervisor as a second year social work student, who would become my supervisor in my first professional position as a clinical social worker at the West Los Angeles VA Medical Center. Emma had already been a mentor to me as a student and we established a warm and effective working relationship.

Emma was everything my mother was not: consistent, kind, loving, complimentary, and appreciative. She taught me to understand and know my grandfather's legacy, how he had influenced my life as a child and also my decisions after his death, and that my own abilities could take me anywhere I wanted to go. She helped me to understand I had something of worth to offer the world. I don't think I ever felt more alive than when I was with her. Looking back I see how much she gave me and how much I owe her.

In another of those what I call "remember when and where moments", I was walking in Westwood Village, going to an appointment after school, midway through my second year of social work school, and I noticed I was walking with a decided spring in my step and with determination and ease. I realised at that moment, halfway across the street on the pedestrian crossing, that I would never again be in a position of subservience in the work environment. I realised that I had something others wanted and I could chart my own course. It was perhaps the most important enlightening moment of my life. I had a career. I had an education. I was marketable. I was good and I had done well in school. I could go anywhere and do anything. I owe those feelings, then and now, to the loving nature of my third surrogate mother, Emma. Unlike my mother and aunt, who was my first surrogate mother, Emma never let me down and we remain close friends now, more than thirty years later. As I continue to embark on new adventures she continues to love me, support me, and encourage me. Sometimes even those of us who have childhoods filled with pain and loss can experience happy outcomes.

USC graduation May 1985 with a masters degree in clinical social work. Ilonka is in the back row on the right.

USC graduation masters degree in clinical social work May 1985.

CHAPTER SEVEN

Boston and the time of my life

In August 1986 I found myself on a plane flying from Los Angeles to Boston after a brief stopover in Reno to visit my mother. My belongings were on a Bekins moving van and my new car was on one of those huge trucks that transport new cars to dealers. This time the new car was mine and moving from LA to Boston, like me.

I remember arriving in Boston late at night, just before midnight. It was hot and steamy at Logan Airport as I waited for my baggage. I was excited and I could feel the heat of the summer on my face. I already had my most important bag, a carry-on with my ten-year-old cat Cinderella. She was allowed in the cabin with me and as we stood waiting for the other luggage—actually I stood and she sat next to me, I wondered to myself, "What in the Sam Hell are you doing here? What are you trying to prove?" I remembered feeling the same thing when I entered Orientation for social work school at USC four years earlier. I also remembered that I had been able to cross those waters successfully. The enormity of what I was undertaking hit me at that moment. Less than a month earlier I was in my condo in Redondo Beach, enjoying my job with the Veterans Association in West Los Angeles and now I was in Boston, my favourite US city, about to begin anew, again. I was eager for it all to begin and a bit fearful as well. How nice it would have been to contact someone for reassurance, but I had nobody.

I remember the taxi ride to the hotel I had booked and where I planned to stay until I could find a place to live. My choice of where to stay was dictated by location and the management's acceptance of pets in the rooms. It was another fateful decision and one that turned out to be one of the best in my life. I got out of the taxi and checked into the place, a mid-sized modest hotel on the north shore of Boston. It was obviously family run and well cared for, too. It was welcoming and the room was large; my cat and I soon felt right at home after a long day and night of travelling across the country.

It was late Saturday night. Sunday morning I wandered downstairs for the complimentary breakfast. It was the day before Labor Day, 1986. The owner was named Tony and he shared his *Boston Globe* newspaper with me. He laid out a tray of sweets and doughnuts. I chose a coconut one and some coffee. He told me that his brother-in-law and sister were co-owners of the hotel with him and that they were looking for a tenant to rent part of their home.

Pat and Tina Santilli owned a two-family home and needed a tenant downstairs in the three bedroom apartment they had recently vacated to move upstairs after a large renovation. Pat was an accountant with an office in Boston and an additional, smaller one, at the hotel as well. Tina was a retired hairdresser and they had one adopted daughter, Corinne, who lived with her husband and family close by in another small town on the north shore. Tony told me that the apartment was not far and took me for a look. The apartment had three bedrooms and was spacious and immaculate. Everything seemed to be falling into place for me and Cinderella. Pat and Tina also loved cats and had one of their own. I immediately said yes to the apartment. I wanted to live with Pat and Tina and they wanted me to live with them. But first they had to check me out. It was unusual for a young woman to travel across the country knowing no one and to start a new job. East Coasters move around less than Californians do and Pat asked for a few personal references before I was actually accepted to move in. I jokingly said to him, "Of course, but you know I will give you the names of people who love me." He laughed, took the names, made the phone calls, and welcomed me with open arms. There and then began a surrogate parent relationship that lasted until April 1992 when I transferred back to California. I never thought I would leave Boston; it was the happiest time in my life. I had finally found myself and felt truly at home. It was in Boston that I first felt competent, smart, confident, and lovable.

A day or two later Pat and Tina moved in a bed, a TV, and some other furniture until I could make arrangements with the Bekins Moving and Storage Company where to deliver my household goods. And, just like that I was a Boston resident.

Labor Day arrived and it was the first sunny weekend after a miserable wet summer. My car arrived as well. I took a drive into town and liked what I saw. I made a trial run to the hospital in Jamaica Plain and drove past some of the historical sites. I was in love and so happy to be in Boston. I was almost giddy with excitement. I began work the following day with enthusiasm and awe. I could hardly believe my good fortune. I was hired by the Social Work Department to work as a clinician on inpatient psychiatry and to also work with veterans with PTSD. My first day was challenging as I was booked to see the family of a recidivist schizophrenic who also had an addiction diagnosis. I quickly settled into my new office and made others feel welcome.

In Boston I easily made friends and by the time my furniture arrived, I had enough friends to invite to my new apartment for a housewarming party. My first true Bostonian friend, a nurse on the unit, Peter Miller, invited me to dinner and soon thereafter I met his fiancée, Janet, over the Thanksgiving weekend. Life was hectic, but I was happy and thrilled to be living in the East. I felt at home.

I did not know my grandfather's history in Boston with the Boston Psychoanalytic Society and Institute many years before although I did know the apartment building on Memorial Drive where he lived and deliberately drove past the building each morning on my way to work. It was as though I continued to feel his presence in my life and in my decision making. It felt as though his hand was on my shoulder, guiding me. He had taught me the importance of working for those less fortunate than ourselves and that was a motivating factor in my career choice of the VA system after the completion of my social work internship. Those values were the ones he learned from his father; they were upper middle class European values. While I had been a strong opponent of the Vietnam War when I was in college, I had respect for those who had been drafted and those who made a choice to join the military. It was the government's policies that I protested, not the young men and women who joined or who were drafted. At that time, and now, I considered that veterans and their families are a vulnerable population.

The first time I heard the words AIDS I was living in California and working at the West Los Angeles VA, just prior to moving to Boston. I knew a bit about it, had many friends who were gay and considered to be high risk, and of course I knew the Rock Hudson story, as I was living in the shadows of Hollywood.

The disclosure of Hudson's AIDS diagnosis provoked widespread public discussion of his homosexual activity. In its August 15, 1985 issue, *People* published a story that discussed his disease in the context of his sexuality. The largely sympathetic article featured comments from famous show business colleagues such as Angie Dickinson, Robert Stack, and Mamie Van Doren, who claimed they knew about Hudson's homosexuality and expressed their support for him. At that time, *People* had a circulation of more than 2.8 million, and as a result of this and other stories, Hudson's homosexuality became fully public. Of course we all know that he tried to hide it due to the fear of rejection and stigma.

After I spent a year in Boston, working on the inpatient psychiatry ward with chronic schizophrenics and depressed veterans, the hospital admitted its first HIV infected young Marine. He presented with symptoms of psychosis that was caused by HIV encephalopathy. HIV-encephalopathy is the result of damage to the brain by long-standing HIV infection. It is also known as HIV-associated dementia, or AIDS-dementia complex. HIV-encephalopathy causes problems with concentration and memory and may cause some slowness of physical movements.

It was not long after this man's admission that I petitioned my department chairman, the hospital director, and the chief of staff to permit me to design a programme for HIV infected veterans. I successfully advocated for a new position to be added in the social work department staff roster and I was the newly designated HIV coordinator. My role was to design, implement, and administer clinically and administratively this new HIV programme which included an outpatient clinic, an inpatient component, and a research component. I was responsible for compiling statistics for the Centers for Disease Control and Prevention, and soon played a major role in Boston-area politics regarding the HIV epidemic and the Department of Veterans Affairs' response to it. A year or two later I applied for Federal Ryan White funding and another social work/case manager position was added to the HIV programme.

Part of my role as HIV coordinator was to reach out to the vulnerable populations in Boston that were affected by the epidemic. That meant taking part in the Boston AIDS Coalition's annual walk to raise money. It also meant becoming involved with the intravenous drug population served by the Lincoln Street Veterans Administration Methadone Clinic. In those days gay and bisexual men constituted 60 per cent of the clinic's population and the other 40 per cent came from those addicted to intravenous drugs and who shared needles in or out of "shooting galleries", supervised injection facilities.

It was through my work in the Boston gay community that I met the president of the Boston Gay, Lesbian and Bisexual Veterans Organization, Cliff Arnesen. He and I became good friends and quickly established a positive working relationship that benefitted both of us and our respective agencies.

Cliff and I worked diligently to promote our programme that soon expanded with new and different components. We designed a Buddy Program and trained people to be assigned to one of the clinic's patients. We started a support group for HIV infected veterans and another group for partners and family members. We designed a case management programme to help secure wraparound services for those who were newly diagnosed through to the end of life. I was appointed chair of the hospital-wide HIV Committee, the first and only time a non-physician sat at the head.

At this time, it was during the early years of the HIV epidemic, fear and suspicion surrounded the diagnosis and illness. A lot of my time was spent travelling throughout the New England states to lecture and speak in order to dispel myths and hopefully diminish the stigma shown to those infected with the virus. Many of my friends and family, less familiar with how the disease was spread, asked if I was afraid. I was unafraid and undeterred and felt as though this programme and tending to these folks was my calling. It was as if my patients had become the children I never had. Many of my patients were estranged from family due to their disease and/or lifestyle. Some were alone at the end of their life and it was common for me to sit with them as death came knocking. I think I must have unconsciously felt their isolation and I wanted to make sure the end of their life was not alone. It always stung that a son, a brother, a husband, or a father was alone and without family at the end. I just did not think that was right. I always thought that nothing was ever so bad that amends could not be made in families. I learned while working with HIV infected veterans that this ideal was not always the case.

Cliff had been very politically active and connected to local politicians long before we met. It was through him in May 1990 that I was invited to join others in Washington DC to testify before Congressman Lane Evans's (Democrat, Illinois) Oversight Committee on Veterans Affairs about the HIV epidemic in Boston and the role of the HIV epidemic at the Boston VA. This is the first time a panel of openly gay men testified before a congressional committee. It was indeed a special and a groundbreaking event and one of which I am extraordinarily proud. This testimony and the other advocating sessions were part of an educational symposium sponsored by the William Joiner Center in Boston who had at the helm House Speaker Tip O'Neill as its Congressional sponsor. Cliff and I met Senator Ted Kennedy, Congressman Barney Frank, and Congressman Gerry Studds on several occasions, all of whom were supportive of the work we were doing. At work I was surrounded by the face of death and disease, but I also had fun and there were happy times. It was for me the best of both worlds.

It was in Boston that I made the conscious decision to leave the Catholic Church. This happened one Sunday morning while I was attending weekly mass. It was near the beginning of my work with HIV infected veterans and the surgeon general of the United States, C. Everett Koop, sent a brochure to each and every home in the country with information about HIV to quell hysteria and fear. The parish priests in Boston were instructed by Cardinal Bernard Law to tell their congregations that they were not allowed to read this information. I sat in the pew, disbelieving what I heard. Not only was this important information to be shared and learned, I really was offended by the Church taking such a hypocritical stance about homosexuality. I sat and thought, "God (or whatever) gave me free will and the ability to think for myself. I think this is rubbish." I got up and walked out of the mass and have not attended mass since that time. I did not know anything at that time, the late

1980s, about my own family's heritage being Jewish. Then and thereafter I felt no need for formal religion.

I totally loved living in Boston. My home environment was perfect as my adoptive/surrogate parents, Pat and Tina, took extremely good care of me and watched over my every need. I often had dinner with them upstairs in their apartment and they entertained me with stories of their early married life and of their families still in the old country. Pat and Tina were Italian and often prepared the traditional Christmas Eve dinner of seven fishes. Although I am of Italian descent, no such tradition took place in the Alexander home. When I remarked inquisitively about this meal, and asked for clarification, Pat would say to me, "Are you sure you're Italian?" We would laugh and laugh about this, year after year. It was like a ritual. He would share some of the traditional food with me, that was all new to me, and I did not like. He was amused and teased me a lot. If there was a bad snow storm in the winter, it would take a long time to get home from work. I had never driven in snow before and the trips were often dangerous and slow. Often I would find a note on my door telling me that dinner was waiting for me upstairs. Anything and everything that I did not have or that I needed was provided to me. They were wonderful to me. I soon grew to love them and they me. The love we shared was as if I was another daughter.

One of the most important relationships, other than the Santillis, to come out of my time in Boston is my friendship with Julia Gunn. Julia is an epidemiologist who was working with me at the VA as the infection control nurse. Her office and mine were adjacent to one other and we would often spend weekends together with friends down on Cape Cod. Julia was from a large family with roots in New Jersey who had come north to attend nursing school in Vermont. She then relocated to Boston and has been there ever since. She now works for the City of Boston Department of Health and is the director of communicable diseases. It was Julia who would years later suggest to me that I research my family and try to learn more about those who came before me. It is she, in fact, who gave me my family. Without Julia I would still be alone.

One weekend on Cape Cod Julia and I went on an early morning beach walk sponsored by the Cape Cod National Seashore in Race Point near Provincetown. The ranger explained many of the birds we saw and he and I began to flirt. We invited him to eat breakfast with us later on that morning and he did join us. The following weekend, and almost every weekend for six years, I went to Cape Cod to see my friend John. He is a marine biologist, also from New Jersey, and an only child. I fell in love with him and I believe he with me. His mother told me more than once that she expected and hoped we would marry. We did not marry and, in fact, John has stayed single. I don't think he was ever able to make a commitment to anyone. When it was time to leave Boston, though I did not want to go, John's failure to make his feelings known to me eased my decision somewhat.

I loved my job. I often say that moving to Boston was the best thing that ever happened to me and that the job in Boston was my most favourite, ever. Since I studied political science, jurisprudence, and constitutional history in college, living in Boston, seeing the landmarks of the Revolution every day, was special to me. Coming from California, where everybody was from somewhere else, and old buildings were torn down for new construction, being in Boston was a dream come true. To see the same buildings that some of the Founding Fathers had lived in and met in was intoxicating to me. To walk in the graveyards and see the graves of Thoreau, Dickinson, Alcott, and others was inspirational. When I first saw Old Ironsides, the *USS Constitution*, turn around in Boston Harbor on the Fourth of July in 1987, as it does every Independence Day, I wept like a little child. I am sentimental and being there, connecting with the past, even though none of my ancestors were part of Boston during those Revolutionary times, awakened in me a sense of permanence and perpetuity that living in Los Angeles never provided. Living in Boston gave me my first real home as an adult. I never wanted to leave Boston. I never planned to leave Boston.

My work as the HIV coordinator in Boston soon became known throughout the entire VA system. One day the chairman of the social work department, John O'Neill, called me into his office. He told me that a chairman of another social work department, in California, expressed interest in me and wanted to offer me a promotion and an opportunity to be mentored and ultimately be a departmental chair as well. John explained to me that this mentor had a long history of training new chairs of the social work department and he had never chosen a female to mentor. I knew then and there that I had no choice but to leave Boston and return to California. If I were to decline, the social work staff in central office in DC would think I was not serious about my career advancement. Everybody knew I was from California and most likely thought I would jump at the chance to return and have all the moving expenses paid. That was not the case; I just did not really want to leave Boston. Ever.

I remember the day I flew out of Boston for the final time. It was March 1992. It was raining cats and dogs. I had my own cat in the carrier beside me in the car as Pat drove me to the airport. My life's belongings had already been picked up by the moving van and I had said a series of very difficult goodbyes over the previous week. I did not want to go. I felt trapped. I had no choice but to leave. I thought I would continue to live in Boston until the end of my life. I remember Pat saying to me during the ride to the airport, "You don't have to go. You can stay here. We love you." But I knew that was not an option. He and Tina did not want me to leave any more than I wanted to go. There was nothing but sadness.

In Boston I had worked hard, achieved success, found something I loved, and returned my skills and talents to those less fortunate than me. I was happy to live these ideals that were impressed upon me in early childhood. Boston provided a new beginning and rebirth to achieve those aspirations. I never wanted to leave Boston any more than I wanted to leave Chadwick twenty-five years earlier. Sometimes decisions are out of our control as was the case in both of these situations.

I cried during the entire flight from Logan to LAX, nearly five hours. When my aunt and uncle met me at the airport, I was grateful to see welcoming faces, but none too happy to be back in California. I knew I belonged in Boston. It was more traditional than California. It was in Boston that I found myself, and for the first time in my life I felt as though I had come home. I believe my grandfather guided me to the best job I ever had and the most wonderful time of my life. Boston combined my love of history, the past, and my hope for a new life. It was in Boston, after all, that my grandfather had spent a year so many decades before. Boston just felt right.

Ilonka with Senator Ted Kennedy and Cliff Arnesen in Washington DC in the spring of 1991. Ilonka and Cliff had testified before a congressional subcommittee on the impact of the HIV epidemic in Boston area veterans a year before.

The two family home where Ilonka lived in Boston for seven years.
Situated on the North Shore.

Ilonka with Senator Ted Kennedy and Cliff Arnesen in May 1990, Washington DC.

Testimony before congressional committee May 1990, Washington DC.

CHAPTER EIGHT

Saying goodbye to the past

I n mid-1992 I returned to California as a supervising
social worker at the Loma Linda Veterans Administration
Medical Center. I found a nice condominium in Redlands,
California but despised the area. Redlands is out in the middle
of nowhere, near the base of the San Bernardino Mountains,
and the Angeles National Forest, more than halfway between
Los Angeles and Palm Springs. It is barren, hot as Hades in the
spring and summer, and more desert-like than I prefer.

The area now occupied by Redlands was originally part
of the territory of the Morongo and Aguas Calientes tribes of
Cahuilla people. The Aguas Caliente also went to settle in Palm
Springs. Expeditions sought to extend Catholic influence to the
indigenous people and the dominion of the Spanish crown into
the area in the 1770s. The site of a tribal meeting was chosen
for a mission outpost. In 1851, the area received its first Anglo
inhabitants with the arrival of several hundred Mormon
pioneers, who had already travelled from Utah and founded
nearby San Bernardino. The Mormons established a prosperous
farming community.

In the 1880s, the arrival of the Southern Pacific and Atchison,
Topeka and Santa Fe railroads, connecting Southern California
to San Francisco and Salt Lake City triggered a land boom,
with speculators such as John W. North flooding the area now

known as the Inland Empire. The Pacific Electric Railway completed an intercity connection between Los Angeles and San Bernardino in 1914, providing a convenient, speedy connection to the fast-growing city of Los Angeles and its new port at San Pedro, bringing greater prosperity to the town and a new role as a vacation destination for wealthy Angelenos.

At the turn of the twentieth century, Redlands was the "Palm Springs" of the next century, with roses being planted along many city streets. The citrus industry declined in the area as more agricultural areas were replaced by suburban estates, and all three citrus packing houses had closed by the end of the 1900s. Today only one packing house remains.

The chairman of the social work department was Steve Petty, a cowboy who wore high-heeled boots to work each day that might just have had spurs for weekend use. He was loud, kind hearted, always dressed in black like Johnny Cash, and Steve thought the world of me. He had worked on the Palo Alto VA inpatient psychiatry ward with Ken Kesey (author of *One Flew over the Cuckoo's Nest*) during the early 1960s and had wonderful stories to tell. He was a smoker and would often ask me or one of the other supervisors to accompany him on a walk that really meant a cigarette break for him. I soon learned not to turn down one of these invites from Steve. It was an opportunity to speak directly to him about ideas and concerns and he often shared personal secrets with me as well. It was a professional and personal bonding experience, those walks with Steve while he smoked.

I enjoyed my time at work and was enrolled in the Social Work Advanced Leadership Training Course (SWALT) that led to another promotion somewhere else in the system as the chair of the social work department. I was eager to gain this promotion and leave the Loma Linda VA that had in its back-yard the Loma Linda University founded on the Seventh-day Adventist religion. I did not feel comfortable in Redlands or in nearby Loma Linda and spent each weekend, after a 200 mile round trip drive, with my cousins or my aunt and uncle, Vicki and Bud. I loved spending time with Ann and Bill and their two young children. Returning on Sunday nights was always depressing for me. The job was great, the environment not so great even though I made a few good friends.

I worked hard, met my career goals, and garnered a respectable reputation among the hospital staff and administration. I was not personally happy though and missed my friends and Boston and took every opportunity to fly east to see them. I flew in one long weekend to celebrate New Year's. I flew to Nova Scotia to see my former Boston friends, Peter and Janet, who moved to Canada in 1990. On one such trip, a year or two later, I met someone who would forever change the course of my life.

Peter and Janet had a long family history of clambakes on Cape Cod and when they moved to Nova Scotia, they continued the tradition. They usually scheduled these beach parties during my visits and on one visit, a friend of theirs attended and played music. He was introduced to me as Graham and I thought him cute and smart. He was also doing some work around their house and garden and I saw him almost daily. He was known by them to be shy and quiet. On the final day of my visit, as I prepared to get into the car for the short ride to the local airport, Graham approached me and asked for a goodbye hug. My friends were stupefied. I said of course and hugged him warmly with what he has since labelled a "California hug". I guess it made an impression on him and we started to write when I got back to California. I think I was smitten and maybe he was too.

In August of 1994, two years after my fateful first meeting with Graham, I returned to Nova Scotia to see friends prior to a two week planned trip to Boston to visit friends and a few days on the Cape to see my former love interest, John. Graham and I connected almost immediately and we spent a lot of time together. I was falling in love with him and knew I would eventually marry him. I left Nova Scotia, went to Boston, and told my friends about him. I returned to work and Graham and I spoke on the phone daily. I flew to Nova Scotia about a month later, for a long weekend in October to celebrate my birthday. I would take a red eye out of LAX on Thursday night, arrive in Boston about sunup, and then take the short flight to Nova Scotia, arriving about 11am. I would then return on Sunday night as Monday was usually a long weekend holiday as I could rest before the start of the week on Tuesday. After a few of these extended weekend trips, Graham proposed marriage to me and I accepted. That particular long weekend, in November 1994, I returned to California feeling euphoric and hopeful about the future, mine, his, and ours together. In retrospect I realise just how impulsive it all was. And it was really ill thought-out as well.

Also during that weekend in Nova Scotia I was interviewed in Yarmouth at the Department of Psychiatry for a new position as administrative and clinical director of a yet-to-open six bed inpatient unit for assessment and short-term treatment of children and adolescents. The hope was to offer these services locally and thus eliminate the need for patients and families to travel four hours to Halifax, the capital city of Nova Scotia, to obtain such care. The administrator informed me after the interview that he would make all the necessary arrangements for Canadian immigration and we agreed I would start work in the New Year, early January 1995. So I returned to California with a fiancé and a new job.

By the autumn of 1994 I had already completed the two year SWALT training at the Loma Linda Veterans Administration Medical Center and was placed on a list of candidates seeking employment as a social work department chair. I allowed that to continue to move forward. I was happy to have concluded the training with distinction and to have solid recommendations from my department chairman, the hospital director, and the chief of staff. When I left the Veterans Administration in late

December 1994, after ten years, I had been accepted as the chair of the social work department of the Syracuse, New York VA Medical Center. I elected to turn down the appointment. I thought that I would be better able to adjust to small town living than would Graham be able to adjust to life in a big city. He was from a very small village and unaccustomed to the hustle and bustle of urban life.

Graham flew to California in mid-December to meet my family and to help me drive back to the East Coast with him to begin our new life together. I found myself leaving California again and wondering if California was the place I would continue to leave, or the place to which I would continue to return. This time I would leave what was familiar to marry for the third time and assume a position with the Department of Health in Nova Scotia at a small rural community hospital. I would marry a man who represented everything I did not have: he is the oldest of six children, from an intact family with close ties to each other and the small community in which they lived. That kind of commitment to each other was new to me and I was quickly seduced and wanted to become a part of it. Again, seeking what I did not have in order to feel part of something, to belong; trying to diminish my sense of being alone.

My best friend through college and into adulthood was a former college room-mate. Despite coming from vastly different socio-economic backgrounds and different life experiences, Pat and I became good friends and remained close friends, best friends, for more than thirty-five years. She was a teacher and I wanted her to come to Nova Scotia and be the maid of honour at our wedding. We chose the Presidents Day weekend in February 1995 because that would allow Pat a long weekend to make the arduous trip. At the last moment she was unable to attend, and my friend Janet, now married to my friend Peter from Boston, stepped in as maid of honour.

Graham and I were married in a friend's home overlooking the Tusket River in rural Yarmouth County during the early evening of February 18, 1995. The atmosphere was cozy and warm as the fire roared and dozens of candles provided the only other light. It was magical as the candlelight flickered against the windowpanes where ice and snow seemed to sparkle outside. Graham's parents and siblings were in attendance and my friend Julia flew in from Boston and brought many bottles of champagne with her for the celebrations.

The morning after the wedding, friends Peter and Janet hosted a brunch in their lovely home overlooking the sea and then Graham and I went to our home in the same village, less than a mile away. By this time I had been working in my new position for nearly two months and I had friends from my many summer trips to visit Peter and Janet and from the clambakes they had on the beach during my visits. I felt optimistic about the future, both at work and at home with Graham, with his family after being so warmly welcomed, and about our place in the community. I considered myself fortunate. Graham had lived in the area for almost ten years before we married so his friends became my friends. All of a sudden I was not alone.

Yarmouth, Nova Scotia is a small port town in the southwest part of the province, across the Bay of Fundy and the Gulf of Maine from Bar Harbor and Portland, Maine. Yarmouth was inhabited originally by the Mi'kmaq who named the region "Keespongwitk", meaning "land's end" due to its geographic isolation being located at the end of a Nova Scotia peninsula.

Samuel de Champlain visited the area back in 1604 and named it "Cap-Fourchu", meaning "forked or cloven cape". The first Europeans to make a settlement on these shores were the French Acadians. New Englanders settled in what is now the town of Yarmouth in 1759; they were from Yarmouth, Massachusetts and they requested that Yarmouth be named after their former home. Yarmouth was founded on June 9, 1761 when a ship carrying three families arrived from Sandwich, Massachusetts.

Through the nineteenth century the town was a major ship-building centre, at one point boasting more registered tonnage per capita than any other port in the world. Yarmouth ships were found in most major ports throughout the world at this time. The town of Yarmouth was incorporated on August 6, 1890. As wooden shipbuilding declined in the late nineteenth century, Yarmouth's shipowners reinvested their capital into factories, iron-hulled steamships, and railways. Those finally were abandoned and today there is ferry connection to Maine as part of the Trans-Canada Highway. The rail service was discontinued about twenty years ago. The Yarmouth of today is mostly a tourist town with many artists in residence, many summer residents from the US, and a large cultural presence with many museums.

Although I knew friends and colleagues from my visiting the Millers on a couple of occasions, I was not prepared for life in this small town. I found the adjustment difficult and long. Many days I would watch CNN, look at my garden, and say to myself inwardly, "This isn't really a foreign country, it is very much like Maine." Of course, Canada is a foreign country and I was not completely comfortable with the changes I had to make in order to feel truly at home. I had romanticised the move to Yarmouth and I had to endure years of teasing and kidding before I was accepted somewhat as a local.

Eventually the bloom fell off the rose, so to speak, and the job became unpleasant. I was accustomed to the rigours of a large bureaucracy and did not understand the workings of local politics in a small town. I was labelled a "come from away" and many of my ideas were flatly discounted because of this designation. I was miserable and most unhappy. A friend working elsewhere in the system knew of my discontent and suggested me as a candidate for a position at the other end of the province in Sydney on Cape Breton Island. The position was to manage a child and adolescent mental health clinic and this clinic was part of a larger network of mental health services in the province. I accepted the position and on January 1, 1999 left my home in Port Maitland with Graham, our cat Cleopatra, and all of our worldly belongings in a large U-Haul truck and drove eight or nine hours to Sydney during a snowstorm to start again, all over again, anew.

We lived in Sydney for a year to get our bearings before we bought our own home. Graham found a rewarding position and began to immerse himself in the local Bahai community. We were happy. I liked my work. I felt fulfilled, respected, and that I was making a difference. I made good connections in the community with other agencies providing services to children and young people and I could see a change in attitudes towards the mental health system because of my work.

My dear aunt Vicki died in 2000 and I travelled back to California to attend the funeral. I promised my cousin that I would return to help her, if and when the family home was to be sold. I did not want Ann to go through all the personal effects alone. We did do that together and her father sold the family home to move closer to her. It was with sadness that I left California. I returned to the East and my work and my life.

In the spring of 2003 I began to receive phone calls from my mother's neighbours in Reno telling me of her erratic behaviour. She had been a smoker for decades and although she had quit ten or more years before this time, she had COPD and her doctor suggested that she required constant oxygen. She chose to not follow the doctor's instructions and because of this, suffered some problems with oxygen depletion causing a psychosis. She was found wandering around outside her home, naked, telling people she was preparing for a job interview on the following day. She was totally incoherent. She had just celebrated her eighty-third birthday and she was living alone having divorced her fifth husband about ten years earlier. She was admitted to the local hospital, and there then began many phone consultations between the social worker and me.

It was determined, rightfully so, that my mother could no longer live alone. A skilled nursing facility seemed to be the best option. She was now experiencing memory difficulties due to self-induced hypoxia and COPD and was in and out of being coherent and "present". She most likely was deemed to be incompetent. I was instructed to fly to Reno in order to sign the official papers for her admission to the nursing home. I did that the Memorial Day weekend in May 2003. When I arrived at the nursing home I was pleasantly surprised by the staff, the appearance of the nursing home and its cleanliness, and the many and varied programmes available for residents. I brought pictures of my father with me from Mama's home as well as a familiar afghan blanket. When she saw me and the photos, she recognised both and called me "one of the Alexander girls".

Seeing her, frail and needy, was a turning point in terms of my feeling compassion for her. All of a sudden I no longer felt intimidated or afraid of her. She was small, she needed help, and I was prepared to do whatever I could for her. After all, she had given me life and my life was good. I owed her at least that much despite our estrangement and our difficult mother-daughter relationship.

My half-sister Marguerita drove from her home to meet me in Reno. That drive was less than three hours. My trip had taken me nearly twenty-four hours to reach my mother. My mother previously asked if she could come and live with Marguerita and this request was denied. I was angry about that. It turned out that that was the least issue I would become angry about.

My mother, because of her narcissism and her splitting behaviour, and long history of a non-existent relationship with her other daughters, always listed me as her sole beneficiary in her will. When she got angry with me over something trivial, she changed her will and left everything to my sister instead. Mama told me for years that she intended to change it back to me but never did so. I assume that her failing health and mental confusion prevented her from making the call to her lawyer and filing a codicil. In any event, when her physician indicated to Mama that she would not recover completely from her condition, and that she should get her affairs in order, Mama wrote out another will, and this one was handwritten. She expressed her wish that her estate be divided equally between her three daughters. It was dated and signed by a witness. I viewed this last minute change as an indication of her attempt to make amends and to change her karma, so to speak. I thought it was an admirable and an important thing for Mama to do and that it should be honoured.

My sister and her husband thought otherwise. Apparently in Nevada two witnesses are required to validate a handwritten will. My mother and her friend did not know that. In the end, my sister, in what I view as her greed to get the money and property, refused to honour my mother's literal dying wish to do something honourable at the end of her life. For that I will never forgive Marguerita. I am not a vengeful person. But in my mind, my sister was entirely wrong. She did not honour our mother. She deliberately did the wrong thing. Not what I would have done. If I had been the sole beneficiary, I would have divided the money/property equally between the three of us. That is the ethical and decent thing to do.

I have skipped ahead in time, but only by a few days as will become apparent. I must return to the nursing home visit and the official papers. I signed the papers, toured the facility, and visited my mother for the two or three days I was in town. On the final day I came to visit she was busy with others in an occupational therapy event. Because I already had a favourable impression of the facility, and knew that my mother may not even know if I had been in to visit as her memory was compromised, I decided to leave and get in the car and drive to LA where my cousins lived. I knew it would be the last time I would see my mother alive. I knew I was leaving her for the final time. I had no regrets whatsoever. I had no guilt. I felt comfortable making this decision and driving away. I am sure I cried a bit but I did enjoy the beauty of the mountains around Lake Tahoe as I drove down into the Sacramento Valley and in to the LA basin. I was happy I made the decision to remove a few sacred items from Mama's house: a pewter engraved mug given to my grandfather by colleagues at the Chicago Institute for Psychoanalysis, a photograph of my grandfather and me walking on the beach in Malibu when I was six or seven, the antique clock given to my grandfather by colleagues in Chicago, and an oil painting done by my great uncle Henry Major that always hung in our home.

My cousin Ann, who is like a sister to me, and her husband Bill were home when I got there. The drive from Reno to LA is about 500 miles and if you concentrate you can make good time, perhaps eight or nine hours. I was tired and grateful to be in the bosom of loved ones. Seeing my mother had been draining and the visit with my half-sister emotionally unrewarding. My sister and I share nothing and it always feels to me like we are strangers. I have always tried to make something of our relationship that really is not there. Ann and Bill and I had some drinks beside the pool and then a lovely dinner outside on the patio under the stars in the late spring warm night air. I felt good. I felt as if I had done my mother proud and had made a good decision regarding her care in the nursing home. We all went to bed late. I was emotionally drained and I was physically tired too from the oppressive heat of Reno and the long drive.

About 7 am, a phone rang. It was the nursing home in Reno and the message was somewhat shocking. Mama had died earlier that morning. There had been no indication that she was on the point of leaving the physical world when I saw her the day before. I was stunned and handed the phone to my cousin Ann. We made arrangements for Mama to be buried in La Jolla where her happiest days were spent. She would be buried in the same cemetery as her parents, in the Holy Cross Catholic Cemetery. My sister was a bit irritated that she was somewhat inconvenienced by my insistence that Mama be buried in La Jolla and not in Reno, closer to her home. I was adamant that Mama be with her parents, my grandparents.

My cousins and I met the mortuary van that transported Mama's body to the cemetery. The driver gave me some personal effects that included a few diamonds. I never told my sister. When my mother began to experience competency issues, she cashed in all my US saving bonds that listed her as a beneficiary. They were purchased prior to my marriage to Graham and totalled in excess of $20,000. I assumed these few diamonds were compensation for what she had taken from me without authorisation or my knowledge.

The gravesite ceremony was brief. I ordered Mama's favourite flowers in her favourite colour: red roses. A local Catholic priest came to recite some prayers over her body. My sister and her two daughters were there and they kept saying they wanted to hurry up and get to Sea World. I was appalled and offended by their behaviour. But my memories and feelings from that day are those of sadness and grief. My mother had died just three months after her eighty-third birthday and was buried with fewer than ten people to see her off on her journey to the spiritual world. I felt tremendous unhappiness and regret for her decisions and her obvious loss of connection to others. It seemed inconceivable to me that one could live for eighty-three years and only ten people attend a funeral. But I think Mama ultimately, and unfortunately, reaped the negative consequences of a sad and lonely life. She was unable to form attachments to others and because of it, went on her final journey alone. I did all that I could to assure a smooth passage. But in the end, it was terribly, terribly sad. I wish it could have been different for her. She deserved it. We all do.

Paradoxically, at that moment I realised that I was smarter than my mother, I was stronger than my mother, and I had made better use of the family resources provided to me than she did.

Then there was another major loss for me. In February 2004, less than four years after Vicki died, and less than a year after my mother died, my beloved Uncle Bud died. He and Vicki had really been my parents for more than thirty years, caring for me, nurturing me, supporting me, and picking up the pieces when I made a major blunder. I felt as though I could not survive without their love and affection. It meant another trip to California and sadness all over again. I began to feel like an orphan once more, alone and without anyone to truly understand me. That is what happens when you grow up as an only child and when you are always on your own. I had no frame of reference with others to make comparisons and share stories.

As the end of my working life began to approach, I felt a need to visit my father for what I knew would be the last time. Throughout the years we had only seen each other from time to time. Although I know that he loved me and our time together was fine, I never called him Dad nor did I have father-daughter feelings for him. My good friend Julia and I drove from Boston down to the Maryland shore to visit my father and stepmother, Janet. We were there less than two hours and my father's dementia was apparent though not total. He appeared to know who I was from time to time and then went to another place and seemed lost in confusion. It was difficult to see this extremely intelligent and accomplished nuclear physicist struggle in such a manner. After all, this was a man who had worked on the Manhattan Project and who had played a pivotal role in the Atomic Energy Commission before it morphed into the Department of Energy. When Julia and I left my father's home she again stressed the importance that I investigate all the genealogical information available about my family.

Graham and I planned to stay in Sydney for five years but my job was gratifying and we remained for ten years instead. However, I was inching closer and closer to the compulsory retirement age in Nova Scotia. The provincial legislature tabled new legislation suggesting that forced retirement at sixty-five was age discrimination but the bill was not passed in time for me to stay at work. I had to leave my position, one that I totally enjoyed. Accordingly, six months before my sixty-fifth birthday, Graham and I bought another home in the town we had left ten years earlier, exactly across the street, and returned to Port Maitland. I was happy to consider rejoining the community I left and to reconnect with friends who had remained loyal during our time away.

The return to Port Maitland was not without its challenges and problems. Leaving work was difficult for me to accept as I knew it would be. I felt as though I had something of value to contribute but I did not know how to do it. I sat alone and contemplated my existence, feeling melancholy and somewhat depressed. The love I felt from friends and Graham's friends, the achievements made in my career, and my overall sense of well-being soon eroded as the old feelings from the past resurfaced. My misgivings about myself were strong and I began to think, I may just have been depressed my whole life. Luckily my grandfather saved me again from the depth of despair. He came to help me in the person of my friend Julia who had suggested I delve into my family history and get answers. She was right but it took me a while to admit her suggestion had credibility. I know now she wanted me to experience family as she had. I know now she loves me unconditionally and wanted me to know that kind of love too. I had lost those feelings of unconditional love when my aunt and uncle died. It felt good to acknowledge them again.

One Friday in late July 2013, my half-brother Mark called me. He and I have the same father, Dr George Rotariu. My father married Mark's mother after my mother divorced him in 1946. He told me that my father had died after a short illness requiring hospitalisation. I did not know he had been ill. I had not been informed. I asked when the funeral would be and my brother made it clear that my attendance was not wanted.

My stepmother refused to allow me to fly to DC to attend the funeral. In fact, my father was hurriedly buried before my California cousins could attend either. None of us was wanted at "this small family affair". Instead, my cousins and I gathered in California and honoured my father who died a month before his ninety-third birthday ourselves. My stepmother crafted an obituary that neither mentioned my father's sister Vicki, her children, or me.

What in the hell is wrong with me? Why doesn't anybody want me around? I knew this was not what my father wanted. This was an especially painful death to accept. This was another funeral from which I was excluded. Just like my grandfather had "rubbed" me out of the picture when my mother married my stepfather, presenting the marriage as if it was her first one, my stepmother rubbed me from the picture and pretended I was not my father's firstborn. I don't understand how she could feel so insecure as to attempt to deny that her husband was previously married when they had a marriage of more than fifty years. I told my brother on the phone that his father was my father also and though it may be inconvenient to concede, it was the reality. I also said, "George would not have wanted this." Mark told me he was just "doing what his mother told him to do". I reassured him that I could recognise his need to be a good son for his mother during her grief. I have never heard from my two half-brothers, my half-sister, or my stepmother since that day although my stepmother soon thereafter sent me my baby book, something my father apparently treasured throughout his life.

When I began to think again of being alone, without anyone, and grasping the enormity that my mother and father, who did not seem to want me, were now dead and gone, I was overcome. For a while I was near a new low, I felt hopeless and helpless. I felt empty and without purpose. I sat alone and cried a lot. While I was not suicidal, I felt miserable and for a long time, too. I tried to quickly shut down those feelings because it meant that my infantile hopes and dreams of a blissful relationship with my parents were also dead and gone. I tried to move on. Because, by then, I had started to meet and know my Broessler/Alexander cousins and that journey, eventually, would stop me from a complete breakdown. Those cousins saved me as well as my grandfather and my need to tell his story and the story of how our lives were linked forever. I had at last found my purpose after retirement, a purpose that turned out to be the real purpose of my life. Everything else had really been only the preface.

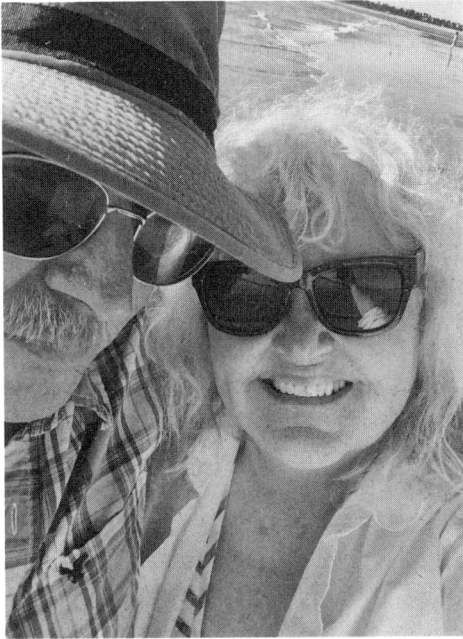

Ilonka and her husband, summer 2016.

CHAPTER NINE

Finding my roots

During a vacation in the spring of 2008 with my friend Julia, an epidemiologist with whom I had worked in Boston decades earlier, I took an early morning boat ride to see the horses on the island of Assateague in the lowlands of Virginia along the Chesapeake Bay. On this particularly beautiful Sunday morning, with the early sun shining on the water and on us, she asked me what I was planning to do when I turned sixty-five in late 2009. I said I had hobbies and she said to me, "I don't think you will sit and do needlepoint." She then suggested to me that a worthwhile hobby was to find out more about my family as I considered myself the last in a line of Alexanders and had grown up without knowledge of any cousins, aunts, or uncles. I always knew intellectually that my grandfather's siblings most likely had children, but I had no information. All this was kept from me. Purposefully and systematically kept from me. As we often do when something uncomfortable is mentioned, I told her "Yes" to keep her quiet without any real intent to follow through.

In the autumn of this same year, Julia sent me a photograph of my great grandfather's grave in the Jewish cemetery in Budapest. It was gnarly and overgrown with vines but clearly one could see the names of my great grandparents, Bernard Alexander and Regina Broessler. I was surprised to learn of the family's Jewish heritage. I told Julia this was news to me and that nobody ever mentioned it to me. She jokingly said, "I think you have to be Jewish to be buried in the Jewish cemetery. You better get accustomed to the idea."

This small bit of information was what I needed to embark on an investigatory path that took about a year to fully complete. I found the email address on the internet of a cousin in Budapest, Zsuzanna Renyi, the granddaughter of my grandfather's younger sister, Borbola, whose name, ironically, was new to me. (I knew the other five names of my grandfather's siblings previously.) I wrote to her and immediately received a reply. Unfortunately, however, she did not contact any other family member to alert them that I was seeking family, and her not doing so caused dissension and anger among those family members who felt valuable time had been lost unnecessarily.

At the end of November 2009 I wrote to a Hungarian professor who had written a scholarly article about my great uncle, Dr Geza Revesz, a Hungarian psychologist who spent most of his academic years in Holland. I expected an automatic reply indicating that the email address was incorrect. Much to my surprise, I received a response with the address in Italy of another cousin, Judit Laqueur-Revesz, who was the daughter of Geza and his wife, Magda, my grandfather's older architect and historian sister.

I wrote to Judit and told her that her mother and my grandfather were siblings. I wrote that I was born in Chicago, grew up in California, and now lived in Nova Scotia across from the state of Maine. I told her I was a psychotherapist and searching for family. I sent off the letter along with a photo but really had minimal expectations. In a week I received a phone call. I immediately fell under the spell of her voice especially when she recited my name, Ilonka, with the exact Hungarian intonation and inflection, what I was accustomed to hearing from my youth. We spoke with ease and love and we agreed that I must come to see her, and soon, as she was at that time ninety-five. After I hung up I was joyful and optimistic about the future.

A week later the phone rang and I could hear my husband speaking again to a cousin. This was not Judit but another cousin she had telephoned to tell of my letter and my story. I began speaking with Eva Broessler Weissman, the daughter of the man who gave my grandfather a microscope to attend medical school. Eva's grandmother and my great grandmother were sisters. Eva told me, now in early December 2009, that I was the best Christmas gift she would ever receive and that she had been looking for me her whole life. She told me she was very family minded and that I must come to Cleveland in the spring, when the roads were better, to meet her. One of the first things Eva asked me was, "Are you Jewish?" I told her no, that I was raised a Roman Catholic as was my mother, her mother, and her father. Eva told me that, "No, you are Jewish." It was a lot to take in. My head began to spin as I started to make plans to travel from Boston to Cleveland as soon as the weather was safe.

Again, the soothing and comforting sound of the European pronunciation of my name was flowing over me. I felt engulfed with love and kindness. I began to understand and know that I was on the cusp of what would become the most important journey of my life. When you do not know where you came from, and the people who came before you, you are alone, and I always seemed to be alone and without direction. Without the past you do not know where to go in the present. But I also began to question why my family had kept me hidden and why the truth had been denied. I knew my mother to be an anti-Semite and my grandmother, too. But I did not understand why or why my cousins had been kept from me and vice versa. I soon began to feel betrayal and anger. This anger would grow for a couple of years while I travelled to meet family all around the world.

Soon after these two life changing phone calls, I placed a call to Julia in Boston and we began to make plans to drive to Cleveland to meet Eva. I soon started writing emails to other cousins, Dr Robin Alexander in Madison, Stella Moore in Dallas, and Dr Vera Alexander (Robin's older sister) in Fairbanks. For about a month Stella and I wrote daily, three or four times daily in fact, and my need for information was insatiable. I realise now I was beginning to feel connected and I wanted and craved more of that feeling. On Valentine's Day that year Stella sent me a book about my great-aunt Magda Revesz Alexander, a book about my great uncle, artist Henry Major, and a jade necklace belonging to her grandmother, my great grandmother, Regina Broessler. She told me that she knew I had nothing belonging to family and that she thought it important that I have these meaningful items. When I looked at the book about Henry Major, I ran into the sitting room and compared the signature on the bottom of a painting that had hung in my home my entire life with those in the book. Little did I know when I removed this painting from my mother's home when she died in 2003 that it was painted by a family member. Again, conflicting emotions flooded over me. I was happy, I was sad, I was discontent, and I was angry. I was grateful and I was scared. I was nervous to consider meeting these cousins and wanted to make sure they would like me. I grew up believing I was unlikeable and unlovable, these feelings the result of my relationship and negative interactions with my own mother, aunt, and grandmother. And, at sixty-five, even after a successful social work career in two different countries, I felt, down deep, that I was unlovable. Despite professional success I had failed to toss away the burden of those early memories and lessons learned in the family.

Eva lived in a high rise condominium building on Lake Erie in Lakeside, Ohio, a suburb of Cleveland. She and her husband, Dr Oscar Weissman, had lived there for decades and Oscar was now dead more than twenty years. The building has two suites for visiting family members to stay in and Eva came down from her upper floor condominium to meet us. I could hear her talking excitedly as she approached us from down the corridor before she reached the doorway. I was scared to death, I was shaking, I was insecure, and hoped to make a good impression. She took one look at me, put her arms around me, and said, "You are family. I love you." Even now, this brings tears to my eyes. I had never been spoken to with such compassion and love. I had never been accepted "just because" without an achievement of some sort. I had known this as a child from my grandfather but even he was results-oriented and had high hopes for me. I had never known love from my mother let alone love of this unconditional kind from her. This exchange was how I entered the warm embrace of the Broessler side of my family and I only received more and more as the meetings continued. I luxuriated in this warmth and it continues to wrap and insulate me now.

Eva and I formed an immediate and intimate bond. We instantly appointed Julia an honorary member of the Broessler clan as she was the principal one responsible for my discovery of cousins around the world with the detection of the photo of Bernard's grave in Budapest. Eva dug through her extensive cupboards and filing cabinets to locate and share important family documents, photos, and mementoes. She regaled us with stories and recollections and the time spent with her went entirely too fast. We were ready to leave to go to Madison to meet up with Robin and Catherine when Eva convinced us to return to Cleveland on our way back home to Boston in order to spend additional time with her. It would be at that time that Eva, Julia, and I created the plan to organise a Broessler family reunion, and decided on La Jolla, my childhood home and where Eva's younger sister Ruth lived, as the meeting place.

Julia and I left Cleveland for Wisconsin, along the I-90 corridor, which would become a familiar route for us over the next three years. We met Robin and his wife Kathy, and Robin gifted us with an unexpected treasure trove. He had in his possession a box of hundreds of old black and white photographs, some very small and taken with the old Minolta cameras so popular in the 1950s and 1960s. The photos were so small that we needed a magnifying glass to enlarge the images. With Julia's help we were able to identify most of the photographs and Robin said he would give them to me to categorise for the entire family. I agreed to scan them and send them to everyone.

On our way back to Cleveland we stopped off to spend a few days in Chicago, my birthplace and the home of my grandfather for more than twenty-five years. A town he always remained fond of and would return to after the final move to California in the mid-1950s. I met Dr David Terman, a psycho-analyst, who was then the director of the Chicago Institute for Psychoanalysis that my grandfather had founded in the autumn of 1932. I sat at his huge and imposing desk and felt right at home. In the library of the institute I shared stories of my family and how I had only recently learned of a Jewish connection. David said to me, "How can that be? Everybody in Chicago knew he was Jewish but nobody spoke about it." I told him that everyone may have known but it was a secret in the family and that the secret was revealed to all my cousins at different times in their lives. It was just revealed to me much later than most.

Chicago has always felt comfortable to me. It is, after all, home and where I was born. My experiences there have always been most positive. During this short stay, Julia and I met Dr Carl Bell, world-famous psychiatrist who was then the director of the Institute for Juvenile Research and had sought me out as Big Papa was once its director, too. We spent a pleasant few hours in the lobby of the hotel, sharing insights, interests, and tales of how we got to this point in our lives. The meeting proved important and serendipitous to me as Carl and I would forge a friendship and I eventually asked him to write the introduction to the biography I wrote about my grandfather, *The Life and Times of Franz Alexander: From Budapest to California.*

* * *

As an aside, soon after returning home, and digesting and processing all the experiences Julia and I had during our initial trip to meet family and make new friends, I told her I was astonished that these accomplished and intelligent people wanted to spend time with me. Underneath it all I still felt unworthy and doubtful. I could not believe this was happening to me. Her response will stick with me, forever. "You don't get it. You attract them." How is it she believed in me, she saw my worth, and I could not? It seems to me now that she must have meant that I was charismatic, interesting, smart, and had something to offer the world. I know I always strived to be those things; I did not and could not accept that I was. The messages of my mother, that I was fat, unappreciative, and that I was not good enough rang forever through my mind. What we say to children and how we treat them, consciously and unconsciously, is so important. I began to consider at this time that I had been a victim of emotional abuse and I started to be angry and sad. I was angry that I had no voice as a child, angry that I had been put through the abuse and that my mother did not love me. But most of all, I felt sad. I felt sad for the little girl inside me who never had the chance to feel a mother's love. I always knew intellectually that none of it was my fault, but felt otherwise. I always felt that if I had tried harder, been prettier, been smarter, been thinner, been better at this or that, that my mother would love me. It was only after meeting Carl in Chicago, and all the other folks I met on the journey that I began, with Julia's help, to understand that my mother did what she could. She herself was working with limited personal resources. My grandfather did what he considered best, for me and for the rest of the family. They were just not good enough and/or wrong. I never thought I could criticise either of them, but I can and my criticism is now tempered with compassion. My sadness continues for myself but also for them.

* * *

Spending time with Eva, on those two short occasions in early 2010, was like the Hallmark greeting card ads on TV at Christmas time. It was joyful, loving, endearing, welcoming, and kind. It was with tremendous sadness that Julia and I left Eva but at least we had a date for the reunion and we could focus on getting together again in the following year. Throughout 2010 I continued non-stop to get to know cousins via email and on the telephone. The overseas telephone calls to my cousin Judit in Italy became more and more frequent and she invited Julia and me to come to see her. I was filled with excitement and glee as I waited for the summer to end and the time of the trip to arrive. During these months I wrote extensively to Nauszika, my cousin Zsuzsanna's daughter, in Budapest, and got to know her. Julia and I decided to combine itineraries and travel to meet them all. We scheduled this to coincide with my sixty-sixth birthday in early October 2010.

The trip to Europe was eye-opening, reaffirming, educational, inspirational, hurtful, and surprising. When I walked the streets of Budapest I felt a connection and a kinship never felt before. I walked the same streets, saw the same buildings that my great grandfather and his family had seen. I felt the past and present come together for me as we stayed in the newly opened New York Palace Hotel that was once the apartment building owned by the New York Life Insurance Company where my great grandparents raised their children. In the café of the building my great grandfather met with other philosophers and students to discuss aesthetics and Shakespeare. From the window of the top floor apartment my grandfather watched Hungary's centennial celebrations and witnessed King Franz

126

Josef pass by. When I took the first section of my grandfather's semi-autobiographical book, *The Western Mind in Transition*, to the manager of the hotel, she told me I was the only relative of a former occupant to meet her. She had met folks whose family had worked in the building when it fell under Communism, but never a resident. I spent my sixty-sixth birthday in the salon eating Hungarian delicacies including dobosh torte, foie gras, and enjoying champagne. The hotel sent me a special sweet to commemorate my birthday which I shared with one of the hotel staff. Through dinner we were serenaded by 1930s and 1940s tunes from the piano bar. It was magical. Budapest had woven a spell around me.

When we went to Italy we travelled to the north country, near the Alps, to see Judit and spend a week with her. At close to 100 years of age, she is the remaining conduit to the people from long ago. She showed us photographs, shared stories and jokes, and thoroughly spellbound us with charm and kindness. Leaving her was most emotional and Julia jokingly said as I cried during the goodbyes, "She does that all the time." Because Judit was ninety-five at the time I thought this would be our only encounter. Luckily for us, I have had two subsequent visits to see her. When I told her of sending an email to Zsuzsi years beforehand, she was angry that this cousin had not made me aware of the other cousins. Judit felt, and still does, that Zsuzsi cheated us of time together. I, too, was a bit angered but tried to focus on what is now and to show gratitude for my good fortune to now have family and forgiveness for others' poor choices. Julia and I spent many days in Venice, walking around the Doge's Palace and the former Venier palace, the Palazzo Venier dei Leoni on the Grand Canal. Connecting with the more familiar Italian roots was enjoyable and fun.

Vera eventually invited me to come to Alaska to meet her and spend time with her and her brother, Robin, whom I met during the initial trip to the Midwest the year before. We all looked forward to getting together at the end of June 2011.

In the meantime Catherine passed away. Vera asked me if I would participate with her, when I was in Alaska, with the scattering of Catherine's ashes into the rivers of Alaska that would eventually take her to the cool waters of the Arctic Ocean. I was moved and said I would be honoured to share in the ritual. I thought maybe this would help to alleviate the sting and pain of the funerals of Big Mama and Big Papa that I had been forbidden to attend. During these days and months Julia would said to me, "This is all good." She never really left my side and wholly understood my wide range of reactions. We were on the phone all the time. Julia has brothers and sisters and their children as her family. I know she wanted those connections to be available for me as well. Her help was the ultimate act of love and kindness to me.

All of a sudden, the most unexpected thing occurred. People seemed as if to come out of the woodwork as new cousins were discovered to live in the United Kingdom, Germany, Australia, the Czech Republic, and Austria, and throughout the US. I think this was the consequence of entering family information on the genealogy website Geni.com—information provided years before to Eva by a distant cousin Jerry Golden in Miami who had previously traced the Broesslers back to the 1700s. Soon our relatively small group of those loyal to the concept of a reunion, that is to come together in Southern California the following year, grew as the plan matured. We continued to make friendships and eagerly awaited in-person meetings. We were dizzy with excitement.

I began to trust these new-found feelings of acceptance and belonging. This was something entirely novel and previously unexperienced. As I began to know my past, and where I had come from, I began to understand where I was going. I began to understand what my life was all about, its purpose if you will. But that road to my future did not really reveal itself until the actual meeting of cousins took place in early July 2011. I did not realise my search for family was a catalyst for many others to do the same thing, work on family genealogy, and then come together as family where they had previously been strangers. I did not know then that I would uncover information about our ancestors; information deliberately obfuscated or lied about beginning in the 1880s. And, in the end, I would discover that many felt what I did: disconnected and alone, lied to, and deliberately kept in the dark. This revelation would come a few years later. For now, even though I was beginning to make connections, I was still largely on my own. Good or bad, that is where I was accustomed to be.

The second time I felt at home while on the journey to family discovery, and at peace, was when I met my cousin Vera in Alaska. Vera is a world-famous oceanographer and is the first woman to obtain a doctorate from the University of Alaska. After a gruelling trip from Boston, and changing planes three or four times, I finally arrived in Fairbanks hours later than anticipated, but Vera was there, waiting for me. Vera and her younger brother Robin met me at the airport and I recognised Robin from the short visit to his home in Wisconsin a year before. On first glance, and for some time after, I could not take my eyes off Vera. She reminded me of my mother and I found myself staring. I knew better. I had, after all, been raised with proper manners in a very traditional home. (Vera is the second of three children born to my grandfather's younger brother, Paul Alexander.) Her colouring, her hair, her height, and petite figure were all a carbon copy of my mother. But her eyes were different and so was her face. While her eyes were precisely the same colour as my mother's eyes, Vera's eyes were kind where I thought my mother's eyes cold and detached. My mother was stern and hard to know. Vera seemed vulnerable, open, and generous. Vera had all the physical attributes of my mother but her presence and her affect were entirely different. Initially it was confusing to me but I soon accepted they were very different people and I fell in love with Vera right then and there.

The three of us spent glorious days exploring part of Alaska and it was then time to fly to La Jolla for the reunion. When we all finally came together I felt whole for the first time ever. The group of cousins became a solid unit and allegiances and alliances were quickly formed spanning generations and time. I felt part of a whole for the first time ever. I learned that many in the family are anxious, like I can be. I learned that many in the family are good cooks, like I am. I learned that many are high achievers, like I am. We even compared feet and found that we all had an elongated second toe. The words "like I am" were not really a part of my being or experience until July 2011. The group who travelled to attend the reunion was about twenty-five strong and as our time together came to a close, we decided to prolong the good feelings the following year in Europe so that the European cousins unable to come to America could participate.

Flying back home with my husband, who had joined us for the party in La Jolla, was a journey I will most likely never forget. I had gone to Alaska and California as an outsider and returned part of something important. The whole is greater than the sum of the parts. I had been connected to people who were my kin. Even though I was angry that they had been kept from me my entire life, and I had lost out on experiences with them during important formative years, I had them now. They were going nowhere and neither was I. I had spent my whole life seeking a place to call home and I had at long last found it, in gold. I was no longer an outsider. I was no longer alone. I was no longer a pariah. I was no longer someone to avoid as my mother had done. I belonged. I was welcomed. I was family. I was loved. Those feelings echoed Eva's words to me the year before when we met for the first time, "You are family. I love you."

The love given openly to me by my Broessler cousins helped to take the hurt away and helped me accept the lies and secrets that had so negatively affected my life. All of a sudden, almost uncharacteristically, I began to see my grandfather as not so perfect. I began to see he was human and, being so, he had made some mistakes regarding choices for me. How I longed to have just fifteen minutes with him now to ask, why did you keep my family from me? Why did you lie and say you did not know where my mother was (and hence, me) when you paid for boarding school and saw us all the time during those years? What did I do to make you decide I was unworthy of knowing my family, my history, and my past? I will never know. I had to come to grips with that and feel only compassion and empathy now. Again, I can say, I am grateful for the bad, and the ugly, for it has brought me here, to the good; the unbelievably good.

To be part of something greater than me, a family, its history, completely turned my life around. It was then that I knew the purpose of my life. When I learned that this wonderful family had been intentionally kept from me, at first I felt anger and confusion. I am still confused but now I feel only empathy and compassion. I am no longer angry. I still do not know the reasons why, but am slowly accepting I may not ever know.

Family reunion La Jolla 2011.

Family reunion New York Palace, Budapest 2012.

Grave of Dr Bernard Alexander and Regina Broessler, Ilonka's great grandparents, Budapest.

CHAPTER TEN

Fulfilling my destiny

What do we mean by destiny and fate? Fate is defined as the events that will necessarily happen to a particular person or thing in the future, as in "She was unable to control her destiny." It is also thought to mean the hidden power believed to control what will happen in the future, your fate: "He believes in destiny." "Your destiny is shaped according to the combination of conditions pre-determined at birth and other factors that you are able to change through your own efforts" (*The Essence of Buddha: The Path to Enlightenment*, by Ryoko Okawa, p. 140: Little, Brown, New York, 2000). It has been in the last few years that I have come to accept my destiny.

I believe that fate brought me to this important place and I am grateful I am no longer afraid. I believe it is essential to embrace what comes to you; that which may eventually bring fulfilment and serenity. Researching the Alexander family, the family of my grandfather, my great grandparents and those before them, making connections, watching as others forged relationships and reconnected with lost relatives, has been the essence of my lifelong search. It is no accident that this has become my life's work. It is no accident I had no real family and realised early on that family was the singularly important element missing in my life. Fate or destiny is often regarded as

135

the "course that life takes" and karma is one of the factors that influence this course. People often believe that fate is predestined and nothing can be changed, but is this really true?

Fate and destiny may have played a role in my move to Boston in 1986 to work for the Boston Veterans Administration Medical Center when, ironically, I already had a perfectly good job working for that same government agency in West Los Angeles. But, through a bureaucratic mistake, fate, I was on a list of people seeking new positions without even knowing it. When the call came to me, I was more than thrilled. I had already formed an attachment to Boston in my mind and when I spent part of the summer of 1981 there, I knew I wanted to live there before my life was over. The other fateful part of that phone call is that I was supposed to be away from the office, travelling to a friend's wedding on the East Coast, and only cancelled my plans earlier that week. Had I been away, as planned, when John O'Neill located my name on the list and called me, and had he found that I was not available to speak to him, he most likely would have gone further down the list to search for a new social worker. Had I not received this phone call, I would not have moved, I would not have met Julia, and she would never have located my family on the internet. If she had not pressed me to find family, to make it my life's work, we would not have found my great grandfather's Jewish heritage, I would not have met any of my cousins, and I most likely would not have written *The Life and Times of Franz Alexander* nor be writing this now.

There was really no reason for me to cancel the trip. I had not had a disagreement with the bride-to-be. The tickets were already purchased. The vacation time had long before been approved by management. I just felt that it would be best for me to remain in Los Angeles that weekend. Did fate keep me from getting on the plane? I believe it did.

Many believe that our fate is decided by a complex combination of circumstances and elements, some even obvious at our birth. Other conditions may come into focus later on during our development yet shape our life, our path, into our future. Carl Jung believed that we choose the family in which to be born and that it is never an accident. I believe that my own fate was determined at birth by the family into which I was born. Perhaps nothing is as important in our karma and development as our own family environment and this is one element that is decided before we are born. Nobody shaped my development as much as my mother and my grandfather. Paradoxically, one may consider that my mother, a cold, rejecting, and abandoning mother, would have provided only a negative experience. And yet I am grateful for she unwittingly taught me self-sufficiency, personal strength, integrity, and also gifted me with intelligence and perseverance. She did not gift me with confidence or the ability to look at my strengths in an objective manner. Because she lacked empathy and the ability to connect unconditionally with others, my relationship to her was an anxious attachment. I never knew what to expect from her. She was always a puzzle to me and I was afraid of her just as I was afraid of my grandmother. I was fortunate that the other major person responsible for my personality structure, for my development, was a doting grandfather who had more time to give me than he had had during his own children's youth when he may have been more concerned about his own image and professional legacy. My grandfather seized the opportunity presented to him by my mother's inherent weaknesses and made sure that my karma would be fulfilled. Through these actions he created my own destiny. All this was done before I was born or in the early weeks after my birth.

Another important component of destiny and karma is the social environment in which we grow and learn. I was fortunate. I had no struggles in terms of the basic needs of life. I had the better things that money and prestige could provide. This element shaping destiny and karma is another that was decided before I was born. We learn and grow through our own efforts and gain self-discipline. Others influence us along the way. For many, spirituality plays an integral role as well.

The most important factor that shapes our fate or destiny is, in fact, the decisions that we make at the turning points in our lives. Our life as it is now is created by the results of the choices we ourselves made according to the tendencies of our own mind, each time we encountered a specific event. It may thus be said that it is none other than freedom of choice which is the most important factor in shaping a person's fate or destiny. Freedom of choice and timing may be the most important components in determining our fate. At least, that is what I have learned from my life's experiences.

We are ultimately totally responsible for our own lives. My mother's choices were poor and that is why at the end of her life, at the age of eighty-three, she was surrounded in death with nobody except nursing home personnel. When she was buried in La Jolla on that June day in 2003, there were fewer than ten people to see her off on her journey. I felt profound sadness but knew at first hand that she had created that fate for herself, years before and in the not so distant past as well. How could there only be just a handful of people who cared that she had died? How sad for her, her entire life, that she never made a real connection with others. My mother was never able to change her fate and accept responsibility for her mistakes. She lived and died alone. I feel nothing but sadness and compassion for her now, more than ten years after her death, that she found neither serenity nor happiness along the way and that she found herself alone in the end, disconnected from what is supposed to bring you happiness—family.

Her greatest gift to me may be her unhappy and unrewarding life and her allowing me to witness it. Of course she never did any of that consciously. In fact, she attempted through estrangement to keep me away for many years. She did not see me during my most formative years, the years between seventeen and thirty-five; from awkward teenager to adulthood. I often

138

thought to myself, how sad for her that the young woman I had become, a successful clinical social worker, had transpired with little of her positive influence or participation. She was never able to break away from making the same mistakes over and over again.

Thanks to the incredible people who entered my life, those surrogate mothers for example, and good friends who have stayed with me for decades, I was able to reflect on my own strengths and weaknesses and to stop making the same mistakes. I was able, with the help of a solid social work graduate school education, and some psychotherapy, to examine my behaviour with a questioning mind and I was able to strive continually to change and seek improvement. I was able to meet and change my fate. I was able later in life, in my thirties, to begin to become the person I was meant to be. The person I believe my grandfather saw and hoped for before I was born. Maybe he saw me as a replacement for his firstborn daughter who was such a disappointment to him.

My starting point occurred when I abandoned the pattern of blaming my mother's lack of love for me for my own unhappiness. After social work school graduation, I decided to undergo a traditional psychoanalysis. I thought it was a good thing to do and thought of it initially as only an intellectual exercise. Freud or my grandfather may have called it resistance. Naturally I called the Southern California Psychoanalytic Institute (now the New Center for Psychoanalysis) and made an appointment. My grandfather was involved in the founding of the institute and its library is named after him. The institute always awards an annual prize in my grandfather's name. I remember going through their assessment protocol and seeing at least three analysts before being assigned an intern. One of the assessors said to me, "You have sad eyes." I realised then and there that I had been found out. I was forced to really take a hard look at my coping and how I had created this web and patina of superficial happiness to protect and guard myself from the sad feelings lurking deep inside me. I wish I could remember who this man was, and I often wonder if he is still alive. I would like to let him know the significance of that statement in terms of turning my life around. I agree with him. I was sad and I continue to feel profound sadness when I allow the past to wash over me like the ocean does the sand at high tide.

However, sadness and anger eventually turned into compassion and forgiveness. Compassion for my mother and her failure to be the mother I wanted her to be. I realise now that we all have an archetype in our mind and in our heart of the mother we want and need. I did not get mine, but then, few of us do. But I did get one very important lesson from Mama that allows me now to forgive her those weaknesses and limitations. That decision, to forgive my mother and move on from the past, also allowed me to trust in the goodness of others and form honest and intimate relationships. This permitted me to trust Julia when she said to me it was important for me to find family. She recognised what was missing in my life and in my soul. It took me a while to actualise a plan, but I built that plan on the trust and the basic foundations of the loving relationship I have with her. Again, had I not been in Los Angeles in August of 1986, when the Boston Veterans Administration staff called me, none of this would have taken place.

Julia and I have spent many hours, too many to count, over the past ten years discussing family, as well as the events that we shared together when we found and met family all around the world. We have gone over conversations and reworked them, again and again, to find another nuance, another clue, to what happened and why. For me, this process has led to an understanding of those who blazed a path for me long before I came into this world. This process allowed me to find peace and serenity but I did not find all the answers. The answers that I want from others will never come, but that is all right with me. The glass is half full and that is sufficient. I have learned to find my own answers, answers that work for me now, and to build on the gifts that others left behind. It just took me a while to figure it all out.

My mother's and grandfather's faults, human frailties, and their weaknesses have ultimately helped me develop compassion and forgiveness. I have never been what one would describe as a resentful person or one that held on to anger for long. I am volatile and can be very emotional. After all, I am Italian as well as Hungarian. Some would say I am highly strung. Anger ends very swiftly for me. I have never seen the benefit of blaming others and hanging on to negativity. So, compassion and forgiveness have been a part of me for a long time. However, the recent gift that my family gave me has been gratitude. As my life has become fuller and richer, as I have been able to meet extraordinary people and achieve successes in my later life, I feel thankfulness for what was given to me. I appreciate the struggles, the disappointments, the pain, and the recovery from it all.

In late 2011, after the initial reunion took place in La Jolla, I decided that my name Ilonka Frances Thomas was no longer a match for me, no longer mirrored who I was in terms of my heritage and ancestry. After all, my Thomas father occupied no part in my life and yet I hung on to his name for decades. After much thought and encouragement from my friend Julia and my cousin Vera, I applied for a name change to better emulate who I am today and who I was at the start of my life: an Alexander. I also wanted to pay tribute to my grandmother and her noble pedigree. Therefore, in January 2012 my name officially became Ilonka Frances Venier Alexander. I wear it with pride and it feels right to me now.

Now, as my grandfather taught me so long ago, it is time to give back to others less fortunate what you yourself have. To that end, I dedicate my life now. But, and in a different way, with a better and deeper understanding of my life's most important lesson.

CHAPTER ELEVEN

A new beginning, at long last

In 2012, after the second Broessler reunion was held, this time in Europe, my task was to write the biography of my grandfather. A biography and tribute that I had thought of doing when I was still an undergraduate student, just after his death in the mid-1960s. It was then, and always was since then, a lofty idea and one that I thought would never really be accomplished.

If there is one single lesson that I have learned throughout the years, it is the lesson of the importance of timing and how that plays a role in decision making and the eventual execution of ideas. The importance of timing first presented itself to me when I made the choice to continue in the field of my Big Papa: mental health and to pursue an education in clinical social work. That decision provided me a pathway to freedom, both financial and professional, and also provided, at long last, that bit of the confidence I so lacked and needed. I realise now just how afraid of failure I was for far too long.

Idries Shah, an Indian writer of philosophy and psychology, said, "Right time, right place, right people equals success. Wrong time, wrong place, wrong people equals most of the real human history." I took that to mean that unless the people, place, and time in your life are in alignment, success will most likely elude you. I had spoken about writing a book many times. The first time was in the 1960s. I put away the idea until 2008 when my friend, confidante, and travelling companion, and honorary Broessler family member, suggested to me, after discovering my family, that there was something important to say. Julia helped to convince me that the timing was right for me to dedicate my energy and talent to such a task.

Another person who convinced me to write the biography was my cousin Vera. I felt as though I had made an instant connection with Vera when I met her in the summer of 2011, as our association grew stronger over time, and when we met again in Europe during the summer of 2012. Vera, Julia, and I travelled in the waning days of summer 2013 to Mackinac, an idyllic island off the coast of Michigan in Lake Huron. Mackinac is situated just a twenty minute ferry ride from the mainland yet is a genuine step back in time. No cars are allowed and transportation other than by horse has not been permitted on the island since the turn of the century. It is as if time stopped in 1910. Such an atmosphere is exactly what I needed to come to grips with my life's most important work. I was beginning to understand that every other accomplishment had been a necessity in order to set the proper timing for this mission.

I spent a week in Mackinac just after Labor Day and I learned another significant lesson from Vera. When we discussed my idea of writing a biography of my grandfather, and I mentioned my fears and insecurities, she helped me realise that the bad conditioning I received was not my fault and I was allowing it to stand in my way of success. She helped me get away from the negative thoughts and fears that were hamstringing me in the writing process. She helped me begin to like myself for really the first time in my life.

She told me that not knowing my family was not my fault. She told me that my mother was emotionally unavailable and no other child would have elicited a different emotional response from my mother. She helped me accept that I was smart, I was intuitive, I was capable of writing something cogent, and capable of getting it published as well. I hold Vera in very high esteem and have for as long as I have known her. She is an extremely accomplished world-renowned scientist with a long and fruitful career in oceanography. She is a shining example to me of what hard work, gutsy determination, and intellect can achieve. When Vera speaks, most listen. I certainly did. Yet when Vera speaks it is with softness and kindness. She does not boast, nor is she bombastic. Vera helped me understand that what I wanted to do, to write a biography of my grandfather, was also good for the family that had just started to make connections with each other. She also helped me see my grandfather as more real and not as idealised as I had held him, as she shared many stories of their relationship over the years.

I returned from my summer vacation in Mackinac, spent with these two extremely smart women, with a new sense of tenacity and purpose. I set about writing, almost daily, and also to find a publisher. I knew that I did not want to self-publish and had my heart set on having the book published by the University of Chicago Press for obvious sentimental reasons. My long-time friend and author, Sandra Phinney, coached me in how to prepare a proposal and I sent it off to Chicago. It seemed a long time before I received an answer and I think it was because the reply was difficult for them to send. I think that they would have wished to publish such a work, but told me in the response that memoirs and biographies are not part of their area of interest. The University of Chicago Press suggested I contact Karnac Books in London. I had not heard of Karnac but when I did my homework, I knew I had found a home. I was fortunate that Karnac believed in my dreams and eventually offered me a contract. I was on cloud nine.

Throughout the spring and summer of 2014 I wrote daily. I researched every manner of details that I could and marvelled at how those before me, accomplished writers, were able to research without the assistance of the internet. I thought of the need to send off letters, perhaps special delivery, and to wait patiently for responses. I enjoyed instant communication and I knew that the kind of patience needed in the past most likely would never be mine.

I recognised that my work would be different from the typical biography of a major psychoanalytic figure in that it was written by a family member whose primary goal was to divulge personal, intimate information. The internet, libraries, psychoanalytic societies, and institutes are full of information about Big Papa's intellect, his contributions, his ideas, and his accomplishments. I wanted to show the personal side of him. I wanted to introduce the family that shaped, motivated, and explained his many decisions made during his twenty-five years at the helm of the Chicago Institute for Psychoanalysis. Remember, my 101-year-old cousin Judit said to me years ago, "He was a hard man to know." I also wanted to weave our story together as he had so greatly impacted my life from the moment of my birth, and the warm arm of his encouragement holds me close to him to this day.

In the autumn of 2014, about a year after the auspicious trip to Mackinac, I sent the manuscript off to Karnac Books and also to my friend, Dr Carl Bell, distinguished US psychiatrist, who had agreed to write an introduction. He was most complimentary about my work and I was happy that someone of his high calibre could see something of value in what I had created. I knew that *The Life and Times of Franz Alexander: From Budapest to California* was to be published as part of the History of Psychoanalysis Series at Karnac Books, whose editors were Dr Brett Kahr and Peter Rudnytsky, both well-known historians and psychoanalysts. What I did not know was that one day in May 2015, my life would change dramatically.

On that morning, while lying in bed, checking my iPhone for emails, I saw an email from Dr Kahr. It contained an introduction and an attachment. He had written a most positive formal introduction to my book (and Dr Carl Bell's introduction became the afterward) and was glowingly encouraging about my work. He mentioned that Karnac Books was interested to conduct a personal interview with me for their companion website Karnacology.com and wondered if I wanted to do this. Naturally I jumped at this unique opportunity.

Brett Kahr and I have become good friends since that time. We are really good friends. He is my confidant, my friend, my mentor. He told me that my book would have a long shelf life and that it would change the course of my life. He told me the book would be a critical and financial success. He said my writing style was compelling, charming, and insightful. I politely said thank you, but did not believe a single word. I have come to see, and experience, however, that since that interview, and subsequent phone calls, and too many emails to tally, Dr Brett Kahr knew of what he spoke. Since the publication of my book in September 2015, my life has been a whirlwind. In fact, after leaving a thirty-year career in clinical social work, both as a clinician and a manager, I see that I am now leading a new and more fulfilling life. Yet again, I have been provided another chance to make a difference and to forge a new start. When I sometimes sit and muse about my good fortune to have such interesting and accomplished people as friends, I am reminded of what Julia said to me once, "You don't get it. You attract these people."

A second book, *Love and Survival in Budapest: The Memoir of Artur Renyi*, has since then been published by Karnac Books. This is a diary written by my great uncle (my grandfather's brother-in-law) and edited by my Budapest cousins and me. It is the story of my grandfather's younger sister's family and their life in Budapest before, during, and after Nazi occupation as Jews. Rachel Shteir wrote about my biography of Big Papa and the subject of bad Freudian fathers in her November 2015 article in the *New Yorker* magazine. My grandfather's house in Palm Springs has since been placed on the US Register of Historical Properties. I was interviewed twice on the radio and interviewed for a newspaper story. I was asked to present a discussion about my book in a series of lunchtime lectures at the Izaak Walter Killam Memorial Library in Yarmouth, Nova Scotia, and this was taped for television. In February 2016 Peter Rudnytsky asked if I would come to the next annual meeting of the American Psychoanalytic Association in Chicago in June 2016 and participate in a discussion of my book and my grandfather's contributions to the field of psychoanalysis. I was asked to come to the Boston Psychoanalytic Society and Institute and be filmed as part of their Meet the Author series in June 2016. While in Boston the institute's librarian asked if I was interested to go through sixty boxes of archival material and "write something". I agreed to do this after this manuscript is finished. Professor Judit Meszaros, noted educator, psychoanalyst, and writer asked if I would come to Budapest and meet with the scholars at the Sandor Ferenczi Society and House and discuss my grandfather and my book. She and I had previously been introduced by Dr Brett Kahr for the express purpose of her writing an introduction to the memoir of Artur Renyi. While in Europe I met up with beloved cousins, and new ones in Italy, and at the meeting in the Sandor Ferenczi House, in the heat of Budapest's summer, I met analysts and psychologists who shared an interest in the work of Franz Alexander. I was welcomed with love and affection and one senior member of the group gave me two first editions of my great grandfather's works in philosophy and aesthetics. I was touched and overwhelmed with emotion. I cried tears of joy and wistfulness and Professor Meszaros put her arm around me and lovingly said, "You brought your grandfather back home to Budapest." She also had tears in her eyes. I was nearly speechless and honoured beyond what words could say.

It was in those moments, in hot and humid Budapest, in a stifling room without air conditioning and with a fever of my own, as I was battling pneumonia and bronchitis, that I felt whole, really whole, for the first time in my life. I felt as though I had finally lived up to the expectations of those who had come before me and those who had unwittingly laid out my life's path for me. I felt then and there, for the first time in my life, that I had accomplished something of importance and that I had finally made my grandfather proud. I felt I was worthy to be known as Alexander's granddaughter.

My grandfather is on my mind a lot these days. He was a great man. Not only to me, not only to the psychoanalytic world, but to all of those who had questioning and creative minds. Throughout my childhood and teen years he taught me the importance of giving to those who were less fortunate. He taught me to become aware of the struggles of others and to do what I could to help. He taught me to question, to learn, and to study. He had seen his own father deny his Jewish heritage because of prejudice and persecution. He had seen the beginnings of Nazism in Germany and had seen what the fascist Arrow Cross government had done to his beloved Hungary and to his own sister and her family. He encouraged me to participate in politics and to volunteer to help get those elected whose values I supported. The roots of my personality and my activism and advocacy come from him.

I believe that this chapter of my life represents rebirth and renewal. If you have not been given the proper foundation as a child, as I was not, it is vital for you to seek it for yourself. When you can rid yourself of the shackles of the past, the pain of the past, and enter into a life of acceptance and peace, you are free. The feelings of being free are now mine. When you are free, good things come to you. That is presently my life and for the first time ever I feel downright gleeful. I am only now beginning to accept my individuality and some of the ways I am special and that I have unique talents. That is what psychological abuse does: it takes away your confidence and it is a long, uphill, demanding battle to reclaim it. As I wrote before, the timing had to be right for me to accept these changes, to continue my work, and to believe in the changes occurring in my life.

I am unsure if there is a heaven or a hell, most likely not. I am unsure if there is a God. I most certainly do not support the Roman Catholic Church any longer. I am beginning to try on the ideas and beliefs of my Jewish heritage as one tries on a pair of new gloves. To see if it all fits into what I want to do now. But what I do know is that my grandfather continues to influence me and I know he is aware of what I have done, both personally and professionally. I have brought his life and mine back to the beginning of our American story. The circle is complete. Chicago in the 1930s, to California in the 1950s, and back again to Chicago and Budapest in 2016. The feelings of being free are now mine. My heart is full.

Franz Alexander, my Big Papa, you were not perfect but you were the perfect father for me. Just as you idealised your own father, so did I idealise and idolise you. You are my Sun King. You and I, we are forever linked together. I am indeed my grandfather's granddaughter. You have not been forgotten and I am happy to say, your legacy lives on.

Ilonka and her husband saying goodbye to their first "exchange daughter" on her way back to France. July 2015.

The home the author shares with her husband in rural Nova Scotia, across the Gulf of Maine from Portland and Bar Harbor. The house was built in 1861 and with Ilonka's loving restoration was designated a heritage property in 2011. It was known as the Maitland Lodge and was the first hotel in the village.